MYTHS AND LEGENDS
OF
CALIFORNIA
AND THE
OLD SOUTHWEST

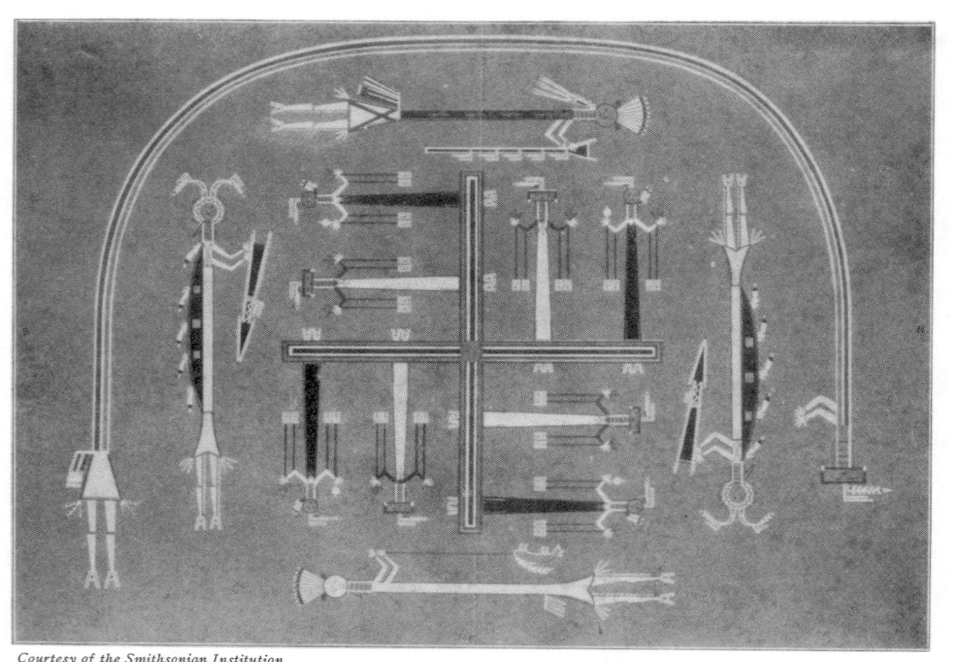

Courtesy of the Smithsonian Institution

ZUNI SAND PAINTING OF "THE SONG HUNTER"
See Explanation p. 137

MYTHS AND LEGENDS
OF
CALIFORNIA
AND THE
OLD SOUTHWEST

COMPILED AND EDITED BY
KATHARINE BERRY JUDSON

Introduction to the Bison Book Edition by
Peter Iverson

ILLUSTRATED

University of Nebraska Press
Lincoln and London

First Bison Book printing: 1994
Most recent printing indicated by the last digit below:
10 9 8 7 6 5 4 3 2 1

Library of Congress Cataloging-in-Publication Data
Judson, Katharine Berry.
Myths and legends of California and the Old Southwest / compiled and edited by Katharine Berry Judson; introduction to the Bison Book edition by Peter Iverson.
p. cm.
Originally published: Chicago : A. C. McClurg & Co., 1912.
"A Bison book."
ISBN 0-8032-7580-3
1. Indians of North America—California—Legends. 2. Indians of North America—Southwest, New—Legends. I. Title.
E78.C15J84 1994
398.2'089970794—DC20
93-46686
CIP

Originally published in 1812 by A. C. McClurg & Co., Chicago.

∞

TABLE OF CONTENTS

Introduction to the Bison Book Edition		1
The Beginning of Newness . .	*Zuni (New Mexico)* . .	19
The Men of the Early Times .	*Zuni (New Mexico)* . .	24
Creation and Longevity . . .	*Achomawi (Pit River, Cal.)*	26
Old Mole's Creation	*Shastika (Cal.)* . . .	27
The Creation of the World . .	*Pima (Arizona)* . . .	29
Spider's Creation	*Sia (New Mexico)* . .	32
The Gods and the Six Regions .	. . . .	36
How Old Man Above Created the World	*Shastika (Cal.)* . . .	37
The Search for the Middle and the Hardening of the World . .	*Zuni (New Mexico)* . .	39
Origin of Light	*Gallinomero (Russian River, Cal.)* . . .	47
Pokoh, the Old Man	*Pai Ute (near Kern River, Cal.)*	48
Thunder and Lightning . . .	*Maidu (near Sacramento Valley, Cal.)* . . .	50
Creation of Man	*Miwok (San Joaquin Valley, Cal.)* . . .	51
The First Man and Woman . .	*Nishinam (near Bear River, Cal.)* . . .	54
Old Man Above and the Grizzlies	*Shastika (Cal.)* . . .	55
The Creation of Man-kind and the Flood	*Pima (Arizona)* . . .	58
The Birds and the Flood . . .	*Pima (Arizona)* . . .	62
Legend of the Flood	*Ashochimi (Coast Indians, Cal.)*	63
The Great Flood	*Sia (New Mexico)* . .	64

TABLE OF CONTENTS

		PAGE
The Flood and the Theft of Fire .	*Tolowa (Del Norte Co., Cal.)*	68
Legend of the Flood in Sacramento Valley	*Maidu (near Sacramento Valley, Cal.)* . . .	70
The Fable of the Animals . . .	*Karok (near Klamath River, Cal.)*	72
Coyote and Sun	*Pai Ute (near Kern River, Cal.)*	75
The Course of the Sun . . .	*Sia (New Mexico)* . .	77
The Foxes and the Sun . . .	*Yurok (near Klamath River, Cal.)*	80
The Theft of Fire	*Karok (near Klamath River, Cal.)*	81
The Theft of Fire	*Sia (New Mexico)* . .	83
The Earth-hardening after the Flood	*Sia (New Mexico)* . .	85
The Origins of the Totems and of Names	*Zuni (New Mexico)* . .	88
Traditions of Wanderings . . .	*Hopi (Arizona)* . . .	89
The Migration of the Water People	*Walpi (Arizona)* . . .	92
Coyote and the Mesquite Beans .	*Pima (Arizona)* . . .	94
Origin of the Sierra Nevadas and Coast Range	*Yokuts (near Fresno, Cal.)*	95
Yosemite Valley and its Indian Names	. . . .	97
Legend of Tu-tok-a-nu′-la (El Capitan)	*Yosemite Valley* . . .	100
Legend of Tis-se′-yak (South Dome and North Dome) . .	*Yosemite Valley* . . .	102
Historic Tradition of the Upper Tuolumne	*Yosemite Valley* . . .	104
California Big Trees	*Pai Ute (near Kern River, Cal.)*	106
The Children of Cloud . . .	*Pima (Arizona)* . . .	107

TABLE OF CONTENTS

		PAGE
The Cloud People	*Sia (New Mexico)*	110
Rain Song	*Sia (New Mexico)*	113
Rain Song		114
Rain Song	*Sia (New Mexico)*	115
The Corn Maidens	*Zuni (New Mexico)*	116
The Search for the Corn Maidens	*Zuni (New Mexico)*	120
Hasjelti and Hostjoghon	*Navajo (New Mexico)*	132
The Song-hunter	*Navajo (New Mexico)*	134
Sand Painting of the Song-hunter	*Navajo*	137
The Guiding Duck and the Lake of Death	*Zuni (New Mexico)*	140
The Boy who Became a God	*Navajo (New Mexico)*	144
Origin of Clear Lake	*Patwin (Sacramento Valley, Cal.)*	151
The Great Fire	*Patwin (Sacramento Valley, Cal.)*	152
Origin of the Raven and the Macaw	*Zuni (New Mexico)*	154
Coyote and the Hare	*Sia (New Mexico)*	157
Coyote and the Quails	*Pima (Arizona)*	160
Coyote and the Fawns	*Sia (New Mexico)*	162
How the Bluebird Got its Color	*Pima (Arizona)*	164
Coyote's Eyes	*Pima (Arizona)*	166
Coyote and the Tortillas	*Pima (Arizona)*	168
Coyote as a Hunter	*Sia (New Mexico)*	170
How the Rattlesnake Learned to Bite	*Pima (Arizona)*	175
Coyote and the Rattlesnake	*Sia (New Mexico)*	178
Origin of the Saguaro and Palo Verde Cacti	*Pima (Arizona)*	182
The Thirsty Quails	*Pima (Arizona)*	184
The Boy and the Beast	*Pima (Arizona)*	185

TABLE OF CONTENTS

		PAGE
Why the Apaches are Fierce	*Pima (Arizona)*	187
Speech on the Warpath	*Pima (Arizona)*	188
The Spirit Land	*Gallinomero (Russian River, Cal.)*	192
Song of the Ghost Dance	*Pai Ute (Kern River, Cal.)*	193

ILLUSTRATIONS

PAGE

Zuni Sand Painting of "The Song Hunter" . . *Frontispiece*
Zuni Sand Altar in Kiva of the North 24
Interior of a Pueblo Zuni House 25
Desert Garden, Showing Cholla, Small Cereus, and Giant Cacti 32
Girl Carrying Water Olla 33
Yuma Indians 36
"When the white man came * * *" 38
"Great towns built on the heights" (Castle of Montezuma) . 39
Yucca Growing through Sand Dune in Tularosa Desert . . 44
Indian Writing 48
Sierra Nevada Mountains 52
Huts of Papago (Pima) Indians, Showing Village Bake-oven . 58
Grand Cañon of the Colorado 62
The Sands of the Desert 63
" * * * so that the waters on the plains flower into Big Waters" (Golden Gate) 70
Fallen Leaf Lake 71
San Luis Rey Mission 74
Sia Ceremonial Vase 84
From the Bell-tower of San Xavier Mission, Tuscon, Arizona 90
Indians in the Grand Cañon 91
Happy Isles. Yosemite 96
A-wai′-a (Mirror Lake) 97
Po′-ho-no (Bridal Veil Falls) 98
Cholok, "the Fall" 99
"Then came the tiny Measuring Worm and began to creep up the rock" (El Capitan) 100
Cathedral Spires 101
Yosemite Valley. Vernal Falls and Nevada Falls from Glacier Point 102

ILLUSTRATIONS

PAGE
" South Dome is the woman and North Dome is the husband " 103
Woh-woh-nau, the Sacred Trees of the Monos 106
Apache Medicine Shirt 107
" The Herati are the floating white clouds * * * " . . 110
" The Heash are clouds like the plains * * * " . . . 111
Zuni Ancestral Rock Gods 116
The Little Basket-maker 124
" On the mountains where the fogs meet " 132
Apache Ollas 133
" * * * in the Northland of cold and white loneliness " 140
Navajo Blanket Weaving 148
Zuni Pueblo from the Southeast 154
Climbing up the Acoma Trail 155
Piñon Tree in the Grand Cañon 158
San Xavier Mission, Tucson, Arizona 159
Mesquite and Small Cereus Cactus 164
Vases with Figures of Butterflies, from Sityatki 165
Sia Masks 172
Palo Verde Cacti 182
Pima Irrigation Dam 183
In the Petrified Forest of Arizona 186
" * * * threw all the Apaches over the mountains " (Apache basket-maker) 187
" Bad Indians go to an island in the Bitter Waters " . . . 192
" The giant Sierras, fringed at the base with dark pines " . . 193

INTRODUCTION

by Peter Iverson

For countless generations Native communities throughout North America have told stories about their worlds. In a time before written forms of communication, the storyteller used both collective memory and individual inspiration to fulfill one of several possible goals. Perhaps it might be to amuse or to instruct or to imagine. Some stories could only be told at certain times of the year. Others could not be told to all members of a village or encampment. But regardless of their purpose or their content, the stories mattered. They reflected values; they imparted lessons. They told how a place, an animal, a people came to be. As with the fables or songs or chants or ballads of different groups around the world, American Indian stories offered much in time to a wider audience curious to learn more about Native history and heritage. Nearly a century ago, Katharine Berry Judson came to understand their importance and sought to share them.

Katharine Berry Judson received a B.A. from Cornell University in 1904. Upon graduation she attended library school in the state of New York and then moved west. Judson served as a librarian in Kalispell, Montana, in 1905 and 1906 and then as chief of the periodical department for the Seattle public library from 1906 until and during the time she enrolled in a graduate program in history at the University of Washington. Awarded the Loretta Denny Fellowship, she completed her M.A. in one year. She then worked as a research assistant in the history department during the

1911–12 year. Somehow she found the time to do work of her own as well, for *Myths and Legends of California and the Old Southwest* emerged in print in 1912. This book, published by A. C. McClurg & Co. of Chicago, lists her as the "author" of three other works, including *Myths and Legends of Alaska* and *Myths and Legends of the Pacific Northwest.* And Judson herself alludes to these "preceding volumes" in her preface. She would go on to compile two other related volumes—*Myths and Legends of the Mississippi Valley and the Great Lakes* and *Myths and Legends of British North America* (about the Indians of North America rather than the British)—all published by McClurg, soon thereafter.

Her interests were not limited to Indian stories. Her master's thesis dealt with "Fur Trading Forts of Old Oregon, 1810–1834" and she also published articles in such varied journals and magazines as the *Oregon Historical Quarterly,* the *American Historical Review,* and *Century Magazine.* Given the limits of opportunity and advancement for American women in the early twentieth century, Ms. Judson clearly was not only bright and ambitious but determined. Her significance may be found in her efforts to find the kind of wide audience merited by Indian stories. So many of the tales had been recounted and transcribed by pioneering ethnologists. But for the average reader in early twentieth century America, Bureau of American Ethnology volumes might as well have been written in Diné (Navajo) as in English. The accounts were buried in volumes not on the usual public library shelves. To make such stories more accessible to the general public proved to be Judson's challenge and ultimately represented her particular contribution. The reprinting of this book by the University of Nebraska Press will make her work in the field of Indian myth better known to another generation of readers.

Judson's experience as a librarian, her graduate training in history, and her residence in the Northwest all obviously affected her work. Then, as now, there existed a tremendous public interest in "traditional" Indian life in the American West. Schoolchildren who trooped into the public libraries of Kalispell and Seattle no doubt quizzed her about many things in regard to American Indians. Realizing the need for more information to be made available to general audiences, she began compiling legends connected with the cultural and physical terrain stretching from Alaska through Oregon before going on to write about California and the Southwest.

Judging from the dates of publication for her books, Judson worked quickly. *Myths and Legends of California and the Old Southwest,* like her other volumes, rested heavily on the pathbreaking work done by late nineteenth- and early twentieth-century linguists and ethnologists who had gathered the tales from members of different American Indian communities. Editor Judson acknowledges "especial credit" due to "the ethnologists whose work has appeared in the publications of the Smithsonian Institution, and the U.S. Geographical and Geological Surveys West of the Rocky Mountains": Mathilda Cox Stevenson, James Stevenson, Frank Hamilton Cushing, Frank Russell, Stephen Powers, James Mooney, and Cosmos Mindeleff. Cushing, Powers, and Mooney, of course, were particularly prominent students of Indian life and Russell, a Pima himself, naturally had special insights and access into the community he recorded. These scholars had done their work in the recent past and Judson must have rejoiced at the chance she had to share their labor with people who would never read a report from the Bureau of American Ethnology or other federal agencies.

The final two decades of the nineteenth century and the first two decades of the twentieth marked a period of intense investigation into the cultures of native North America. Anthropologists and others believed themselves in a rather desperate race against the corrosive tides of rapid assimilation. Thus, photographer Edward Curtis tried to capture what he deemed the essence of Indian life before it vanished altogether, entitling one of his most heralded photographs "The Vanishing Race." More recent research has revealed how Curtis staged the nature of the image he tried to create; if some vestige of more contemporary life crept in, Curtis erased it in the darkroom. Such a preoccupation with some kind of aboriginal purity makes us appreciate Judson's reference to "the quainter, purer myths," even if the label today strikes us as false and inappropriate.

Judson must also have been driven by the kind of working assumption that inspired sculptor James Fraser's statue "The End of the Trail." As several students of Indian history have observed, this image of the slumped warrior on horseback attested to a kind of inevitable decay and decline of Indian America that had to attend the continued ascension of industrial America. If the stories weren't collected now, they would disappear. If the Field Museum of Chicago and other such institutions did not go out to collect and appropriate cultural artifacts, including those of religious significance, they would not be visible for future generations to appreciate.

In the final years of this century, it is easy to look back and scoff or be appalled by such efforts. There are far more Indians in the United States today than there were in Judson's time. Native communities now understandably want the return, sooner rather than later, of objects of social and sacred significance purchased, borrowed, or stolen from them years ago. Many of the tribal languages remain, although television and urbanization have taken their toll. And many of the stories are still told, either in similar or altered form. Moreover, there are new stories that have been generated since Judson's era. Without justifying or condemning the conduct of any turn-of-the-century ethnologist or anthologist, it is fair to conclude that they misjudged the staying power of Indians. But, given the rapid demographic growth of non-Indian populations in the early 1900s and the precarious nature of Indian land holdings, we can see why they did so.

Then, too, Anglo-Americans may have not comprehended how new technology could augment Native culture rather than serve as a recipe for instant deterioration. The Indians of Judson's own Northwest Coast provide a nice example. Did access to new metal tools with which they could carve and shape wood more quickly and easily mean that Indian carving would abruptly decline? In fact, the production of what outsiders called totem poles increased in number and in complexity, thanks to technological change. New technology thus allowed for innovation and creativity; it did not automatically prompt cultural disintegration.

Of course, we should not be shocked that early-twentieth-century observers did not have our advantage of hindsight. Ethnologists such as James Mooney at least had the gumption to testify before congressional committees in favor of religious freedom for Indians who used peyote in the Native American Church. And they did do essential work in what was undeniably a transitional era. If Mooney had not gone out to western Nevada to interview Wovoka, our overall understanding would not have been enhanced of the movement known to us simply, if misleadingly, as the Ghost Dance. If Mooney had not labored with the calendar history of the Kiowas, then the Kiowa writer of a later generation, N. Scott Momaday, would not have been able to employ that labor so beautifully in *The Way to Rainy Mountain.* And if Mooney and the others had not tried so hard to learn so much in this turbulent and traumatic time, then it is reasonable to assume that some stories, some teachings, some lessons might well have been lost.

Judson paid the ethnologists the kind of tribute less likely to be accorded in our own time. She sometimes took whole paragraphs or more directly from her sources and used them without any kind of editing. In other instances she only modified slightly the wording. The longer and the more complicated the account, the more likely her red or blue editorial pencil was used. She acknowledged the work of the ethnologists in her preface and named names. One can retrace her steps today and see her use of a Frank Cushing or a Frank Russell. It is clear she is not trying to hide her debt; she just did not feel it necessary to encumber the book with specific citations her readers usually would not find of interest or import.

From today's vantage point, we would prefer her editorial stance to be that of Stith Thompson, the distinguished professor of English and folklore at Indiana University, who published *Tales of the North American Indians* in 1929. Professor Thompson also acknowledged "the untiring labors of a score or two of field workers" and also sought to serve "the general reader" who, without access to journals and other technical publications, wanted "without undue expenditure of time to acquaint himself with American Indian tales." He cited in each instance the exact source of the stories included in his collection. And he was willing to allow for adaptation and incorporation. After chapters of mythological stories, mythological incidents, trickster tales, hero tales, journeys to the other world, animal wives, and husbands, and miscellaneous tales (to employ his titles), Thompson includes a chapter of "tales borrowed from Europeans" and a brief concluding chapter of four Indian versions of Bible stories. Thompson's readers probably liked reading about the Zuni version of Cinderella and the Cherokee rendition of the tar baby. But Judson evidently saw her audience as well as her task a little differently. Just as today more popular writers have little patience with scholars who chide them about their lack of footnotes or proper citation,

Judson might have seen such quarrels as quibbles. What mattered, she might have muttered, was the story itself.

Her organization and selection of these tales, to be sure, reflect her own conscious, deliberate choices as an editor. As she had just plowed neighboring geographical ground, she is more intrigued by Arizona and New Mexico than California. Of her stories, nearly two-thirds hail from the Southwest. One is tempted to suggest that this may just be an early example of a person from the Seattle area casting aspersions on California, but Judson was hardly alone in her particular fascination with such peoples as the Navajos, the Pimas, or the residents of the Pueblo communities of Arizona and New Mexico. I recall being encouraged during schooldays in California to make pueblo villages out of milk cartons and not being particularly prompted to learn much at all about the Native peoples of my own native state. Even now the Indian heritage of California remains largely invisible in an ever more urban state, while large, visible nations such as the Navajos continue to be highlighted in the public imagination. Go to the headquarters of that quintessential California magazine, *Sunset,* in the town where I grew up and what do you observe? Navajo rugs.

Judson's very label, "the Old Southwest," smacks of romanticism, a kind of Charles Lummis-like appreciation of a sleepy yet culturally vibrant world of land and time enough. Clearly, she is quite taken with its peoples, whom she has recently discovered, so to speak. One is surprised only by her limited inclusion of the Hopis, perhaps the most idealized of all Indian nations in the Southwest, and her omission of other pueblo groups such as Acoma. However, one must assume that Judson had to go with what she had; some of the major anthropological work remained to be done at Hopi, and Acoma's twentieth-century prominence has had as much to do with its pottery as its magnificent site. In 1912, Acoma pottery, like other Pueblo pottery, had yet to enjoy the kind of renaissance it would experience in the 1920s with the extraordinary artistry of San Ildefonso potter Maria Martinez being unveiled through the commercial interests along the Santa Fe railroad line. Judson's decision to include the Apaches only once and then in a less than positive light through a Pima story ("Why the Apaches Are Fierce") betrays both the long shadow of Geronimo and the general popular image of the Apaches in the early twentieth century, as well as the fact that anthropologists such as Morris Opler had yet to complete their work.

In this book, the editor has chosen to include mostly stories about creation and origins, as well as a sampling of tales about that ubiquitous figure, Coyote. Other animals and birds appear here: the hare, quail, fawn, rattlesnake, raven. It is important for us to understand the significance of place, of the land itself, and of other creatures on the land in these accounts. In telling the stories, Indians spoke to the central significance of place. This is where we began, the stories may say. This is where we belong. This is where we should be. We are on the land, but we do not possess the land. We are on the land, but we do not control it, nor do we have priority over other beings. Indeed, what the stories tell us now, just as they told Native audiences generations ago, is the inter-related fate of people with the earth and all of its occupants. And the stories tell us the importance of proper conduct and the perils of behaving badly. Actions and thoughts have consequences, the stories say. They cannot be made to disappear with a casual "sorry about that" or some other less than heartfelt dismissal of responsibility. If you jump in the water and the water is too deep, you will drown. Just like Coyote.

In somewhat the same way that collectors for the Field Museum might be amazed today to see that many of the treasures they acquired are now at long last being returned to their homes in Native communities, so, too, Katharine

Berry Judson might not fully have anticipated the fate of the stories she acquired, or more accurately, condensed and recycled. In many instances, they are still being told in the Indian nations. For example, the story told by Pima elder Anna Moore Shaw in *Pima Indian Legends* (published in 1968 by the University of Arizona Press and in print today) about Coyote and the Quails is the same Pima story included in this volume. In many other instances, new stories have been invented. The Coyote of Leslie Marmon Silko, the modern storyteller from Laguna Pueblo, is not at all the Coyote we see here. And although Silko's Coyote is a direct descendant of the Coyote that Judson chose not to include, the being Karl Luckert has called "excrement-corpse-fool-gambler-imitator-trickster-witch-hero-savior-god" (see introductory essay to *Navajo Coyote Tales* by Father Berard Haile, O.F.M., Bison Book, 1984) the essential lessons to be drawn from the Coyote brought to us by the editor do not appear to differ dramatically.

Since the time of Judson and Stith Thompson, the stories have continued to command a considerable audience, both Indian and otherwise. In fact, one could argue that it is larger than in 1912. University presses have reprinted much of the work of ethnologists such as Frank Cushing and Stephen Powers. And new collections, either newly collected or newly retold, such as Barry Holstun Lopez, *Giving Birth to Thunder, Sleeping with His Daughter: Coyote Builds North America* (1977), or Richard Erdoes and Alfonso Ortiz, *American Indian Myths and Legends* have not disappointed their publishers. Such popularity attests to the ability of new storytellers. But as with the advent of the widely beloved storytellers in clay inaugurated by Helen Cordero of Cochiti Pueblo, the stories do build upon older foundations. Cordero's inspiration for her original storyteller, say Barbara A. Babcock and Guy and Doris Monthan in *The Pueblo Storyteller* (University of Arizona Press, 1986, pages 21–23) came from her grandfather, Santiago Quintana. Santiago Quintana was a storyteller whose words were recorded by ethnologists Adolph Bandelier and Ruth Benedict of the late nineteenth and early twentieth century. And yes, Edward Curtis took many photographs of Mr. Quintana.

So, in similar and different forms, the stories continue to be told, just as the Navajos continue to weave, maintaining traditional styles but also inventing new ones as well as returning to recreate patterns popular a century ago. Katharine Berry Judson, no doubt, would approve. She did her part to perpetuate the stories, by placing oral accounts in a lasting, written form. And she would have agreed, I think, that there is always room for a new character in the stories, for there are always new lessons to be learned, new beings to be fooled or taught, and old and new places to be appreciated or seen from a different perspective. Perhaps we can look forward to new stories about the Spotted Owl.

September 1993

PREFACE

IN the beginning of the New-making, the ancient fathers lived successively in four caves in the Four-fold-containing-earth. The first was of sooty blackness, black as a chimney at night time; the second, dark as the night in the stormy season; the third, like a valley in starlight; the fourth, with a light like the dawning. Then they came up in the night-shine into the World of Knowing and Seeing.

So runs the Zuni myth, and it typifies well the mental development, insight, and beauty of speech of the Indian tribes along the Pacific Coast, from those of Alaska in the far-away Northland, with half of life spent in actual darkness and more than half in the struggle for existence against the cold and the storms loosed by fatal curiosity from the bear's bag of bitter, icy winds, to the exquisite imagery of the Zunis and other desert tribes, on their sunny plains in the Southland.

It was in the night-shine of this southern land, with its clear, dry air and brilliant stars, that the Indians, looking up at the heavens above them, told the story of the bag of stars — of Utset, the First Mother, who gave to the scarab beetle, when the floods came, the bag of Star People, sending him first into the world above. It was a long climb to the world above and the tired little fellow, once safe, sat down by the sack. After a while he cut a tiny hole in the bag, just to see what was in it, but the Star People flew out and filled the heavens everywhere. Yet he saved a few stars by grasping the neck of the sack, and sat there, frightened and sad, when Utset, the First Mother, asked what he had done with the beautiful Star People.

The Sky-father himself, in those early years of the New-making, spread out his hand with the palm downward, and into all the wrinkles of his hand set the semblance of shining yellow corn-grains, gleaming like sparks of fire in the dark of the early World-dawn. "See," said Sky-father to Earth-mother, "our children shall be guided by these when the Sun-father is not near and thy mountain terraces are as darkness itself. Then shall our children be guided by light." So Sky-father created the stars. Then he said, "And even as these grains gleam upward from the water, so shall seed grain like them spring up from the earth when touched by water, to nourish our children." And he created the golden Seed-stuff of the corn.

PREFACE

It is around the beautiful Corn Maidens that perhaps the most delicate of all imagery clings, Maidens offended when the dancers sought their presence all too freely, no longer holding them so precious as in the olden time, so that, in white garments, they became invisible in the thickening white mists. Then sadly and noiselessly they stole in amongst the people and laid their corn wands down amongst the trays, and laid their white broidered garments thereon, as mothers lay soft kilting over their babes. Even as the mists became they, and with the mists drifting, fled away, to the far south Summer-land.

Then began the search for the Corn Maidens, found at last only by Paiyatuma, the god of dawn, from whose flute came wonderful music, as of liquid voices in caverns, or the echo of women's laughter in water vases, heard only by men of nights as they wandered up and down the river trail.

When he paused to rest on his journey, playing on his painted flute, butterflies and birds sought him, and he sent them before to seek the Maidens, even before they could hear the music of his song-sound. And the Maidens filled their colored trays with seed-corn from their fields, and over all spread broidered mantles, broidered with the bright colors and the creature signs of the Summer-land, and thus following him, journeyed only at night and dawn, as the dead do, and the stars also.

Back to the Seed People they came, but only to give to the ancients the precious seed, and this having been given, the darkness of night fell around them. As shadows in deep night, so these Maidens of the Seed of Corn, the beloved and beautiful, were seen no more of men. But Shutsuka walked behind the Maidens, whistling shrilly as they sped southward, even as the frost wind whistles when the corn is gathered away, among the lone canes and the dry leaves of a gleaned field.

The myths of California, in general, are of the same type as those given in a preceding volume on the myths of the Pacific Northwest. Indeed many of the myths of Northern Californian tribes are so obviously the same as those of the Modocs and Klamath Indians that they have not been repeated. Coyote and Fox reign supreme, as they do along the entire coast, though the birds of the air take a greater part in the creation of things. These stories are quaint and whimsical, but they lack the beauty of the myths of the desert tribes. There is nothing in all Californian myths, so far as I have studied them, which in any way compares with the one of the Corn Maidens, referred to above, or the Sia myths of the Cloud People.

PREFACE

In the compilation of this volume, the same idea has governed as in the two preceding volumes — simply the preparation of a volume of the quainter, purer myths, suitable for general reading, authentic, and with illustrations of the country portrayed, but with no pretensions to being a purely scientific piece of work. Scientific people know well the government documents and reports of learned societies which contain myths of all kinds, good, bad, and indifferent. But the volumes of this series are intended for popular use. Changes have been made only in abridgments of long conversations and of ceremonial details which detracted from the myth as a myth, even though of great ethnological importance.

Especial credit is due in this volume to the work of the ethnologists whose work has appeared in the publications of the Smithsonian Institution, and the U. S. Geographical and Geological Surveys West of the Rocky Mountains: to Mrs. Mathilda Cox Stevenson for the Sia myths, and to the late James Stevenson for the Navajo myths and sand painting; to the late Frank Hamilton Cushing for the Zuni myths, to the late Frank Russell for the Pima myths, to the late Stephen Powers for the Californian myths, and also to James Mooney and Cosmos Mindeleff. The recent publications of the

University of California on the myths of the tribes of that State have not been included.

Thanks are also due to the Smithsonian Institution for the illustrations accredited to them, to the Carnegie Institution of Washington for illustrations from the Desert Botanical Laboratory at Tucson, Arizona, and to Mr. Ferdinard Ellerman of the Mount Wilson Observatory and to others.

K. B. J.

Department of History,
University of Washington.

MYTHS AND LEGENDS
OF
CALIFORNIA
AND THE
OLD SOUTHWEST

MYTHS AND LEGENDS OF

CALIFORNIA AND THE OLD SOUTHWEST

THE BEGINNING OF NEWNESS

Zuni (New Mexico)

BEFORE the beginning of the New-making, the All-father Father alone had being. Through ages there was nothing else except black darkness.

In the beginning of the New-making, the All-father Father thought outward in space, and mists were created and up-lifted. Thus through his knowledge he made himself the Sun who was thus created and is the great Father. The dark spaces brightened with light. The cloud mists thickened and became water.

From his flesh, the Sun-father created the Seed-stuff of worlds, and he himself rested upon the waters. And these two, the Four-fold-containing Earth-mother and the All-covering Sky-father, the surpassing beings, with power of changing their forms even as smoke changes in the wind, were the father and mother of the soul-beings.

Then as man and woman spoke these two together. "Behold!" said Earth-mother, as a great terraced bowl appeared at hand, and within it water, "This shall be the home of my tiny children. On the rim of each world-country in which they wander, terraced mountains shall stand, making in one region many mountains by which one country shall be known from another."

Then she spat on the water and struck it and stirred it with her fingers. Foam gathered about the terraced rim, mounting higher and higher. Then with her warm breath she blew across the terraces. White flecks of foam broke away and floated over the water. But the cold breath of Sky-father shattered the foam and it fell downward in fine mist and spray.

Then Earth-mother spoke:

"Even so shall white clouds float up from the great waters at the borders of the world, and clustering about the mountain terraces of the horizon, shall be broken and hardened by thy cold. Then will they shed downward, in rain-spray, the water of life, even into the hollow places of my lap. For in my lap shall nestle our children, man-kind and creature-kind, for warmth in thy coldness."

So even now the trees on high mountains near the clouds and Sky-father, crouch low toward Earth-mother for warmth and protection. Warm is Earth-mother, cold our Sky-father.

Then Sky-father said, "Even so. Yet I, too, will be helpful to our children." Then he spread his hand out with the palm downward and into all the wrinkles of his hand he set the semblance of shining yellow corn-grains; in the dark of the early world-dawn they gleamed like sparks of fire.

"See," he said, pointing to the seven grains between his thumb and four fingers, "our children shall be guided by these when the Sun-father is not near and thy terraces are as darkness itself. Then shall our children be guided by lights." So Sky-father created the stars. Then he said, "And even as these grains gleam up from the water, so shall seed grain like them spring up from the earth when touched by water, to nourish our children." And thus they created the seed-corn. And in many other ways they devised for their children, the soul-beings.

But the first children, in a cave of the earth, were unfinished. The cave was of sooty blackness, black as a chimney at night time, and foul. Loud became their murmurings and lamentations, until many sought to escape, growing wiser and more man-like.

But the earth was not then as we now see it. Then the Sun-father sent down two sons (sons also of the

Foam-cap), the Beloved Twain, Twin Brothers of Light, yet Elder and Younger, the Right and the Left, like to question and answer in deciding and doing. To them the Sun-father imparted his own wisdom. He gave them the great cloud-bow, and for arrows the thunderbolts of the four quarters. For buckler, they had the fog-making shield, spun and woven of the floating clouds and spray. The shield supports its bearer, as clouds are supported by the wind, yet hides its bearer also. And he gave to them the fathership and control of men and of all creatures. Then the Beloved Twain, with their great cloud-bow lifted the Sky-father into the vault of the skies, that the earth might become warm and fitter for men and creatures. Then along the sun-seeking trail, they sped to the mountains westward. With magic knives they spread open the depths of the mountain and uncovered the cave in which dwelt the unfinished men and creatures. So they dwelt with men, learning to know them, and seeking to lead them out.

Now there were growing things in the depths, like grasses and vines. So the Beloved Twain breathed on the stems, growing tall toward the light as grass is wont to do, making them stronger, and twisting them upward until they formed a great ladder by which men and creatures ascended to a second cave.

Up the ladder into the second cave-world, men and the beings crowded, following closely the Two Little but Mighty Ones. Yet many fell back and were lost in the darkness. They peopled the under-world from which they escaped in after time, amid terrible earth shakings.

In this second cave it was as dark as the night of a stormy season, but larger of space and higher. Here again men and the beings increased, and their complainings grew loud. So the Twain again increased the growth of the ladder, and again led men upward, not all at once, but in six bands, to become the fathers of the six kinds of men, the yellow, the tawny gray, the red, the white, the black, and the mingled. And this time also many were lost or left behind.

Now the third great cave was larger and lighter, like a valley in starlight. And again they increased in number. And again the Two led them out into a fourth cave. Here it was light like dawning, and men began to perceive and to learn variously, according to their natures, wherefore the Twain taught them first to seek the Sun-father.

Then as the last cave became filled and men learned to understand, the Two led them forth again into the great upper world, which is the World of Knowing and Seeing.

THE MEN OF THE EARLY TIMES

Zuni (New Mexico)

EIGHT years was but four days and four nights when the world was new. It was while such days and nights continued that men were led out, in the night-shine of the World of Seeing. For even when they saw the great star, they thought it the Sun-father himself, it so burned their eye-balls.

Men and creatures were more alike then than now. Our fathers were black, like the caves they came from; their skins were cold and scaly like those of mud creatures; their eyes were goggled like an owl's; their ears were like those of cave bats; their feet were webbed like those of walkers in wet and soft places; they had tails, long or short, as they were old or young. Men crouched when they walked, or crawled along the ground like lizards. They feared to walk straight, but crouched as before time they had in their cave worlds, that they might not stumble or fall in the uncertain light.

When the morning star arose, they blinked excessively when they beheld its brightness and cried out

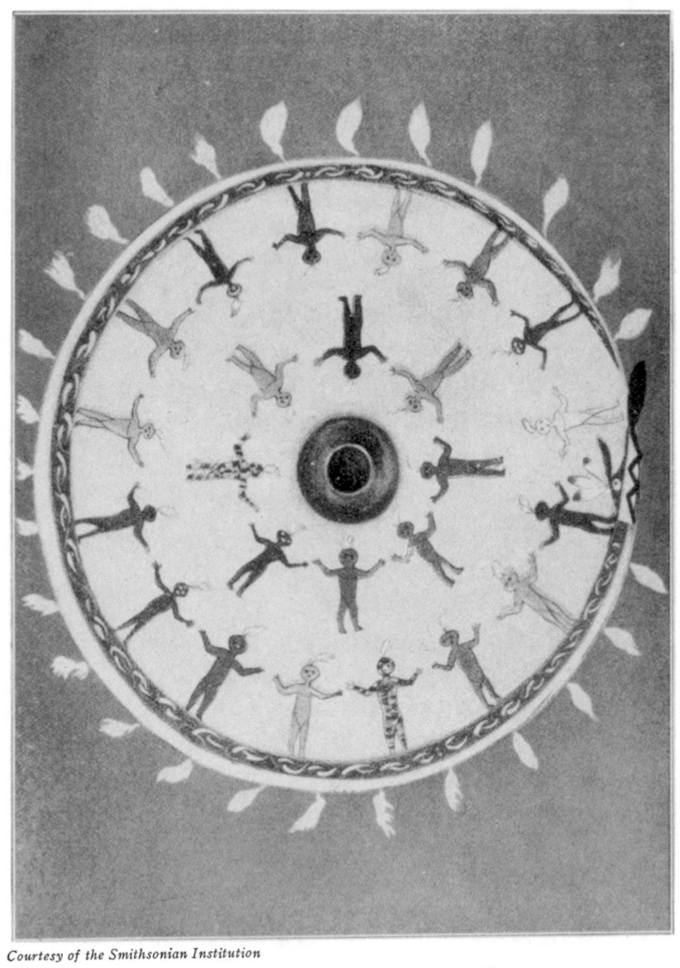

Courtesy of the Smithsonian Institution

ZUNI SAND ALTAR IN KIVA OF THE NORTH

Interior of a Pueblo Zuni House

that now surely the Father was coming. But it was only the elder of the Bright Ones, heralding with his shield of flame the approach of the Sun-father. And when, low down in the east, the Sun-father himself appeared, though shrouded in the mist of the world-waters, they were blinded and heated by his light and glory. They fell down wallowing and covered their eyes with their hands and arms, yet ever as they looked toward the light, they struggled toward the Sun as moths and other night creatures seek the light of a camp fire. Thus they became used to the light. But when they rose and walked straight, no longer bending, and looked upon each other, they sought to clothe themselves with girdles and garments of bark and rushes. And when by walking only upon their hinder feet they were bruised by stone and sand, they plaited sandals of yucca fibre.

CREATION AND LONGEVITY

Achomawi (Pit River, Cal.)

COYOTE began the creation of the earth, but Eagle completed it. Coyote scratched it up with his paws out of nothingness, but Eagle complained there were no mountains for him to perch on. So Coyote made hills, but they were not high enough. Therefore Eagle scratched up great ridges. When Eagle flew over them, his feathers dropped down, took root, and became trees. The pin feathers became bushes and plants.

Coyote and Fox together created man. They quarrelled as to whether they should let men live always or not. Coyote said, "If they want to die, let them die." Fox said, "If they want to come back, let them come back." But Coyote's medicine was stronger, and nobody ever came back.

Coyote also brought fire into the world, for the Indians were freezing. He journeyed far to the west, to a place where there was fire, stole some of it, and brought it home in his ears. He kindled a fire in the mountains, and the Indians saw the smoke of it, and went up and got fire.

OLD MOLE'S CREATION

Shastika (*Cal.*)

LONG, long ago, before there was any earth, Old Mole burrowed underneath Somewhere, and threw up the earth which forms the world. Then Great Man created the people. But the Indians were cold.

Now in the east gleamed the white Fire Stone. Therefore Coyote journeyed eastward, and brought back the Fire Stone for the Indians. So people had fire.

In the beginning, Sun had nine brothers, all flaming hot like himself. But Coyote killed the nine brothers and so saved the world from burning up. But Moon also had nine brothers all made of ice, like himself, and the Night People almost froze to death. Therefore Coyote went away out on the eastern edge of the world with his flint-stone knife. He heated stones to keep his hands warm, and as the Moons arose, he killed one after another with his flint-stone knife, until he had slain nine of them. Thus the people were saved from freezing at night.

When it rains, some Indian, sick in heaven, is weeping. Long, long ago, there was a good young Indian on earth. When he died the Indians wept so that a flood came upon the earth, and drowned all people except one couple.

THE CREATION OF THE WORLD

Pima (Arizona)

IN the beginning there was nothing at all except darkness. All was darkness and emptiness. For a long, long while, the darkness gathered until it became a great mass. Over this the spirit of Earth Doctor drifted to and fro like a fluffy bit of cotton in the breeze. Then Earth Doctor decided to make for himself an abiding place. So he thought within himself, "Come forth, some kind of plant," and there appeared the creosote bush. He placed this before him and set it upright. But it at once fell over. He set it upright again; again it fell. So it fell until the fourth time it remained upright. Then Earth Doctor took from his breast a little dust and flattened it into a cake. When the dust cake was still, he danced upon it, singing a magic song.

Next he created some black insects which made black gum on the creosote bush. Then he made a termite which worked with the small earth cake until it grew very large. As he sang and danced upon it, the flat world stretched out on all sides until it was as large as it is now. Then he made a round sky-cover to fit over it, round like the houses of the Pimas. But the earth shook and stretched, so that it was unsafe. So Earth Doctor made a gray spider which was to spin a web around the edges of the earth and sky, fastening them together. When this was done, the earth grew firm and solid.

Earth Doctor made water, mountains, trees, grass, and weeds — made everything as we see it now. But all was still inky blackness. Then he made a dish, poured water into it, and it became ice. He threw this round block of ice far to the north, and it fell at the place where the earth and sky were woven together. At once the ice began to gleam and shine. We call it now the sun. It rose from the ground in the north up into the sky and then fell back. Earth Doctor took it and threw it to the west where the earth and sky were sewn together. It rose into the sky and again slid back to the earth. Then he threw it to the far south, but it slid back again to the flat earth. Then at last he threw it to the east. It rose higher and higher in the sky until it reached the highest point in the round blue cover and began to slide down on the other side. And so the sun does even yet.

Then Earth Doctor poured more water into the dish and it became ice. He sang a magic song, and threw the round ball of ice to the north where the earth and sky are woven together. It gleamed and shone, but not so brightly as the sun. It became the moon, and it rose in the sky, but fell back again, just as the sun had done. So he threw the ball to the west, and then to the south, but it slid back each time to the earth. Then he threw it to the east, and it rose to the highest point in the sky-cover and began to slide down on the other side. And so it does even to-day, following the sun.

But Earth Doctor saw that when the sun and moon were not in the sky, all was inky darkness. So he sang a magic song, and took some water into his mouth and blew it into the sky, in a spray, to make little stars. Then he took his magic crystal and broke it into pieces and threw them into the sky, to make the larger stars. Next he took his walking stick and placed ashes on the end of it. Then he drew it across the sky to form the Milky Way. So Earth Doctor made all the stars.

SPIDER'S CREATION

Sia (New Mexico)

IN the beginning, long, long ago, there was but one being in the lower world. This was the spider, Sussistinnako. At that time there were no other insects, no birds, animals, or any other living creature.

The spider drew a line of meal from north to south and then crossed it with another line running east and west. On each side of the first line, north of the second, he placed two small parcels. They were precious but no one knows what was in them except Spider. Then he sat down near the parcels and began to sing. The music was low and sweet and the two parcels accompanied him, by shaking like rattles. Then two women appeared, one from each parcel.

In a short time people appeared and began walking around. Then animals, birds, and insects appeared, and the spider continued to sing until his creation was complete.

But there was no light, and as there were many people, they did not pass about much for fear of treading upon each other. The two women first created

Department of Botanical Research of the Carnegie Institution of Washington

DESERT GARDEN, SHOWING CHOLLA, SMALL CEREUS, AND GIANT CACTI

Copyrighted by George Wharton James

GIRL CARRYING WATER OLLA

were the mothers of all. One was named Utset and she was the mother of all Indians. The other was Now-utset, and she was the mother of all other nations. While it was still dark, the spider divided the people into clans, saying to some, "You are of the Corn clan, and you are the first of all." To others he said, "You belong to the Coyote clan." So he divided them into their clans, the clans of the Bear, the Eagle, and other clans.

After Spider had nearly created the earth, Ha-arts, he thought it would be well to have rain to water it, so he created the Cloud People, the Lightning People, the Thunder People, and the Rainbow People, to work for the people of Ha-arts, the earth. He divided this creation into six parts, and each had its home in a spring in the heart of a great mountain upon whose summit was a giant tree. One was in the spruce tree on the Mountain of the North; another in the pine tree on the Mountain of the West; another in the oak tree on the Mountain of the South; and another in the aspen tree on the Mountain of the East; the fifth was on the cedar tree on the Mountain of the Zenith; and the last in an oak on the Mountain of the Nadir.

The spider divided the world into three parts: Ha-arts, the earth; Tinia, the middle plain; and Hu-wa-ka, the upper plain. Then the spider gave to these People of the Clouds and to the rainbow, Tinia, the middle plain.

Now it was still dark, but the people of Ha-arts made houses for themselves by digging in the rocks and the earth. They could not build houses as they do now, because they could not see. In a short time Utset and Now-utset talked much to each other, saying,

"We will make light, that our people may see. We cannot tell the people now, but to-morrow will be a good day and the day after to-morrow will be a good day," meaning that their thoughts were good. So they spoke with one tongue. They said, "Now all is covered with darkness, but after a while we will have light."

Then these two mothers, being inspired by Sussistinnako, the spider, made the sun from white shell, turkis, red stone, and abalone shell. After making the sun, they carried him to the east and camped there, since there were no houses. The next morning they climbed to the top of a high mountain and dropped the sun down behind it. After a time he began to ascend. When the people saw the light they were happy.

When the sun was far off, his face was blue; as he came nearer, the face grew brighter. Yet they did not see the sun himself, but only a large mask which covered his whole body.

The people saw that the world was large and the country beautiful. When the two mothers returned to the village, they said to the people, "We are the mothers of all."

The sun lighted the world during the day, but there was no light at night. So the two mothers created the moon from a slightly black stone, many kinds of yellow stone, turkis, and a red stone, that the world might be lighted at night. But the moon travelled slowly and did not always give light. Then the two mothers created the Star People and made their eyes of sparkling white crystal that they might twinkle and brighten the world at night. When the Star People lived in the lower world they were gathered into beautiful groups; they were not scattered about as they are in the upper world.

THE GODS AND THE SIX REGIONS

IN ancient times, Po-shai-an-ki-a, the father of the sacred bands, or tribes, lived with his followers in the City of Mists, the Middle Place, guarded by six warriors, the prey gods. Toward the North, he was guarded by Long Tail, the mountain lion; West by Clumsy Foot, the bear; South by Black-Mark Face, the badger; East by Hang Tail, the wolf; above by White Cap, the eagle; below by Mole.

So when he was about to go forth into the world, he divided the earth into six regions: North, the Direction of the Swept or Barren Plains; West, the Direction of the Home of the Waters; South, the Place of the Beautiful Red; East, the Direction of the Home of Day; upper regions, the Direction of the Home of the High; lower regions, the Direction of the Home of the Low.

Putnam & Valentine

Yuma Indians

HOW OLD MAN ABOVE CREATED THE WORLD

Shastika (*Cal.*)

LONG, long ago, when the world was so new that even the stars were dark, it was very, very flat. Chareya, Old Man Above, could not see through the dark to the new, flat earth. Neither could he step down to it because it was so far below him. With a large stone he bored a hole in the sky. Then through the hole he pushed down masses of ice and snow, until a great pyramid rose from the plain. Old Man Above climbed down through the hole he had made in the sky, stepping from cloud to cloud, until he could put his foot on top the mass of ice and snow. Then with one long step he reached the earth.

The sun shone through the hole in the sky and began to melt the ice and snow. It made holes in the ice and snow. When it was soft, Chareya bored with his finger into the earth, here and there, and planted the first trees. Streams from the melting snow watered the new trees and made them grow. Then he gathered the leaves which fell from the trees and blew upon them.

They became birds. He took a stick and broke it into pieces. Out of the small end he made fishes and placed them in the mountain streams. Of the middle of the stick, he made all the animals except the grizzly bear. From the big end of the stick came the grizzly bear, who was made master of all. Grizzly was large and strong and cunning. When the earth was new he walked upon two feet and carried a large club. So strong was Grizzly that Old Man Above feared the creature he had made. Therefore, so that he might be safe, Chareya hollowed out the pyramid of ice and snow as a tepee. There he lived for thousands of snows. The Indians knew he lived there because they could see the smoke curling from the smoke hole of his tepee. When the pale-face came, Old Man Above went away. There is no longer any smoke from the smoke hole. White men call the tepee Mount Shasta.

Putnam & Valentine

"When the White Man came . . ."

Putnam & Valentine

"Great Towns Built in the Heights" (Castle of Montezuma)

THE SEARCH FOR THE MIDDLE AND THE HARDENING OF THE WORLD

Zuni (New Mexico)

AS it was with the first men and creatures, so it was with the world. It was young and unripe. Earthquakes shook the world and rent it. Demons and monsters of the under-world fled forth. Creatures became fierce, beasts of prey, and others turned timid, becoming their quarry. Wretchedness and hunger abounded and black magic. Fear was everywhere among them, so the people, in dread of their precious possessions, became wanderers, living on the seeds of grass, eaters of dead and slain things. Yet, guided by the Beloved Twain, they sought in the light and under the pathway of the Sun, the Middle of the world, over which alone they could find the earth at rest.[1]

When the tremblings grew still for a time, the people paused at the First of Sitting Places. Yet they were still poor and defenceless and unskilled, and the

[1] The earth was flat and round, like a plate.

world still moist and unstable. Demons and monsters fled from the earth in times of shaking, and threatened wanderers.

Then the Two took counsel of each other. The Elder said the earth must be made more stable for men and the valleys where their children rested. If they sent down their fire bolts of thunder, aimed to all the four regions, the earth would heave up and down, fire would belch over the world and burn it, floods of hot water would sweep over it, smoke would blacken the daylight, but the earth would at last be safer for men.

So the Beloved Twain let fly the thunderbolts.

The mountains shook and trembled, the plains cracked and crackled under the floods and fires, and the hollow places, the only refuge of men and creatures, grew black and awful. At last thick rain fell, putting out the fires. Then water flooded the world, cutting deep trails through the mountains, and burying or uncovering the bodies of things and beings. Where they huddled together and were blasted thus, their blood gushed forth and flowed deeply, here in rivers, there in floods, for gigantic were they. But the blood was charred and blistered and blackened by the fires into the black rocks of the lower mesas.[1] There were

[1] Lava.

vast plains of dust, ashes, and cinders, reddened like the mud of the hearth place. Yet many places behind and between the mountain terraces were unharmed by the fires, and even then green grew the trees and grasses and even flowers bloomed. Then the earth became more stable, and drier, and its lone places less fearsome since monsters of prey were changed to rock.

But ever and again the earth trembled and the people were troubled.

"Let us again seek the Middle," they said. So they travelled far eastward to their second stopping place, the Place of Bare Mountains.

Again the world rumbled, and they travelled into a country to a place called Where-tree-boles-stand-in-the-midst-of-waters. There they remained long, saying, "This is the Middle." They built homes there. At times they met people who had gone before, and thus they learned war. And many strange things happened there, as told in speeches of the ancient talk.

Then when the earth groaned again, the Twain bade them go forth, and they murmured. Many refused and perished miserably in their own homes, as do rats in falling trees, or flies in forbidden food.

But the greater number went forward until they came to Steam-mist-in-the-midst-of-waters. And they saw the smoke of men's hearth fires and many houses scattered over the hills before them. When they came nearer, they challenged the people rudely, demanding who they were and why there, for in their last standing-place they had had touch of war.

"We are the People of the Seed," said the men of the hearth-fires, "born elder brothers of ye, and led of the gods."

"No," said our fathers, "we are led of the gods and we are the Seed People. . . ."

Long lived the people in the town on the sunrise slope of the mountains of Kahluelawan, until the earth began to groan warningly again. Loath were they to leave the place of the Kaka and the lake of their dead. But the rumbling grew louder and the Twain Beloved called, and all together they journeyed eastward, seeking once more the Place of the Middle. But they grumbled amongst themselves, so when they came to a place of great promise, they said, "Let us stay here. Perhaps it may be the Place of the Middle."

So they built houses there, larger and stronger than ever before, and more perfect, for they were strong in numbers and wiser, though yet unperfected as men. They called the place "The Place of Sacred Stealing."

Long they dwelt there, happily, but growing wiser and stronger, so that, with their tails and dressed in the skins of animals, they saw they were rude and ugly.

In chase or in war, they were at a disadvantage, for they met older nations of men with whom they fought. No longer they feared the gods and monsters, but only their own kind. So therefore the gods called a council.

"Changed shall ye be, oh our children," cried the Twain. "Ye shall walk straight in the pathways, clothed in garments, and without tails, that ye may sit more straight in council, and without webs to your feet, or talons on your hands."

So the people were arranged in procession like dancers. And the Twain with their weapons and fires of lightning shored off the forelocks hanging down over their faces, severed the talons, and slitted the webbed fingers and toes. Sore was the wounding and loud cried the foolish, when lastly the people were arranged in procession for the razing of their tails.

But those who stood at the end of the line, shrinking farther and farther, fled in their terror, climbing trees and high places, with loud chatter. Wandering far, sleeping ever in tree tops, in the far-away Summerland, they are sometimes seen of far-walkers, long of tail and long handed, like wizened men-children.

But the people grew in strength, and became more perfect, and more than ever went to war. They grew vain. They had reached the Place of the Middle.

They said, "Let us not wearily wander forth again even though the earth tremble and the Twain bid us forth."

And even as they spoke, the mountain trembled and shook, though far-sounding.

But as the people changed, changed also were the Twain, small and misshapen, hard-favored and unyielding of will, strong of spirit, evil and bad. They taught the people to war, and led them far to the eastward.

At last the people neared, in the midst of the plains to the eastward, great towns built in the heights. Great were the fields and possessions of this people, for they knew how to command and carry the waters, bringing new soil. And this, too, without hail or rain. So our ancients, hungry with long wandering for new food, were the more greedy and often gave battle.

It was here that the Ancient Woman of the Elder People, who carried her heart in her rattle and was deathless of wounds in the body, led the enemy, crying out shrilly. So it fell out ill for our fathers. For, moreover, thunder raged and confused their warriors, rain descended and blinded them, stretching their bow strings of sinew and quenching the flight of their arrows as the flight of bees is quenched by the sprinkling plume of the honey-hunter. But they devised bow

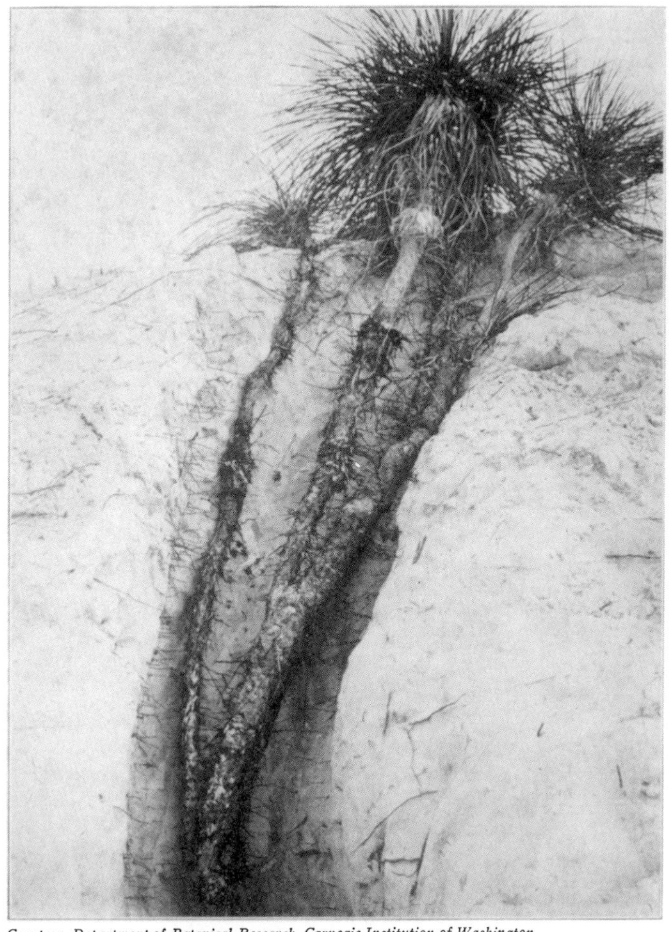

Courtesy, Department of Botanical Research, Carnegie Institution of Washington

YUCCA GROWING THROUGH SAND DUNE IN TULAROSA DESERT

strings of yucca and the Two Little Ones sought counsel of the Sun-father who revealed the life-secret of the Ancient Woman and the magic powers over the under-fires of the dwellers of the mountains, so that our enemy in the mountain town was overmastered. And because our people found in that great town some hidden deep in the cellars, and pulled them out as rats are pulled from a hollow cedar, and found them blackened by the fumes of their war magic, yet wiser than the common people, they spared them and received them into their next of kin of the Black Corn. . . .

But the tremblings and warnings still sounded, and the people searched for the stable Middle.

Now they called a great council of men and the beasts, birds, and insects of all kinds. After a long council it was said,

"Where is Water-skate? He has six legs, all very long. Perhaps he can feel with them to the uttermost of the six regions, and point out the very Middle."

So Water-skate was summoned. But lo! It was the Sun-father in his likeness which appeared. And he lifted himself to the zenith and extended his fingerfeet to all the six regions, so that they touched the north, the great waters; the west, and the south, and the east, the great waters; and to the northeast the waters above. and to the southwest the waters below. But to the north his finger foot grew cold, so he drew it in. Then gradually he settled down upon the earth and said, "Where my heart rests, mark a spot, and build a town of the Mid-most, for there shall be the Mid-most Place of the Earth-mother."

And his heart rested over the middle of the plain and valley of Zuni. And when he drew in his finger-legs, lo! there were the trail-roads leading out and in like stays of a spider's nest, into and from the mid-most place he had covered.

Here because of their good fortune in finding the stable Middle, the priest father called the town the Abiding-place-of-happy-fortune.

ORIGIN OF LIGHT

Gallinomero (Russian River, Cal.)

IN the earliest beginning, the darkness was thick and deep. There was no light. The animals ran here and there, always bumping into each other. The birds flew here and there, but continually knocked against each other.

Hawk and Coyote thought a long time about the darkness. Then Coyote felt his way into a swamp and found a large number of dry tule reeds. He made a ball of them. He gave the ball to Hawk, with some flints, and Hawk flew up into the sky, where he touched off the tule reeds and sent the bundle whirling around the world. But still the nights were dark, so Coyote made another bundle of tule reeds, and Hawk flew into the air with them, and touched them off with the flints. But these reeds were damp and did not burn so well. That is why the moon does not give so much light as the sun.

POKOH, THE OLD MAN

Pai Ute (near Kern River, Cal.)

POKOH, Old Man, they say, created the world. Pokoh had many thoughts. He had many blankets in which he carried around gifts for men. He created every tribe out of the soil where they used to live. That is why an Indian wants to live and die in his native place. He was made of the same soil. Pokoh did not wish men to wander and travel, but to remain in their birthplace.

Long ago, Sun was a man, and was bad. Moon was good. Sun had a quiver full of arrows, and they are deadly. Sun wishes to kill all things.

Sun has two daughters (Venus and Mercury) and twenty men kill them; but after fifty days, they return to life again.

Rainbow is the sister of Pokoh, and her breast is covered with flowers.

Lightning strikes the ground and fills the flint with

Putnam & Valentine

INDIAN WRITING

fire. That is the origin of fire. Some say the beaver brought fire from the east, hauling it on his broad, flat tail. That is why the beaver's tail has no hair on it, even to this day. It was burned off.

There are many worlds. Some have passed and some are still to come. In one world the Indians all creep; in another they all walk; in another they all fly. Perhaps in a world to come, Indians may walk on four legs; or they may crawl like snakes; or they may swim in the water like fish.

THUNDER AND LIGHTNING

Maidu (near Sacramento Valley, Cal.)

GREAT-MAN created the world and all the people. At first the earth was very hot, so hot it was melted, and that is why even to-day there is fire in the trunk and branches of trees, and in the stones.

Lightning is Great-Man himself coming down swiftly from his world above, and tearing apart the trees with his flaming arm.

Thunder and Lightning are two great spirits who try to destroy mankind. But Rainbow is a good spirit who speaks gently to them, and persuades them to let the Indians live a little longer.

CREATION OF MAN

Miwok (San Joaquin Valley, Cal.)

AFTER Coyote had completed making the world, he began to think about creating man. He called a council of all the animals. The animals sat in a circle, just as the Indians do, with Lion at the head, in an open space in the forest. On Lion's right was Grizzly Bear; next Cinnamon Bear; and so on to Mouse, who sat at Lion's left.

Lion spoke first. Lion said he wished man to have a terrible voice, like himself, so that he could frighten all animals. He wanted man also to be well covered with hair, with fangs in his claws, and very strong teeth.

Grizzly Bear laughed. He said it was ridiculous for any one to have such a voice as Lion, because when he roared he frightened away the very prey for which he was searching. But he said man should have very great strength; that he should move silently, but very swiftly; and he should be able to seize his prey without noise.

Buck said man would look foolish without antlers.

And a terrible voice was absurd, but man should have ears like a spider's web, and eyes like fire.

Mountain Sheep said the branching antlers would bother man if he got caught in a thicket. If man had horns rolled up, so that they were like a stone on each side of his head, it would give his head weight enough to butt very hard.

When it came Coyote's turn, he said the other animals were foolish because they each wanted man to be just like themselves. Coyote was sure he could make a man who would look better than Coyote himself, or any other animal. Of course he would have to have four legs, with five fingers. Man should have a strong voice, but he need not roar all the time with it. And he should have feet nearly like Grizzly Bear's, because he could then stand erect when he needed to. Grizzly Bear had no tail, and man should not have any. The eyes and ears of Buck were good, and perhaps man should have those. Then there was Fish, which had no hair, and hair was a burden much of the year. So Coyote thought man should not wear fur. And his claws should be as long as the Eagle's, so that he could hold things in them. But no animal was as cunning and crafty as Coyote, so man should have the wit of Coyote.

Then Beaver talked. Beaver said man would have

Putnam & Valentine

Sierra Nevada Mountains

to have a tail, but it should be broad and flat, so he could haul mud and sand on it. Not a furry tail, because they were troublesome on account of fleas.

Owl said man would be useless without wings.

But Mole said wings would be folly. Man would be sure to bump against the sky. Besides, if he had wings and eyes both, he would get his eyes burned out by flying too near the sun. But without eyes, he could burrow in the soft, cool earth where he could be happy.

Mouse said man needed eyes so he could see what he was eating. And nobody wanted to burrow in the damp earth. So the council broke up in a quarrel.

Then every animal set to work to make a man according to his own ideas. Each one took a lump of earth and modelled it just like himself. All but Coyote, for Coyote began to make the kind of man he had talked of in the council.

It was late when the animals stopped work and fell asleep. All but Coyote, for Coyote was the cunningest of all the animals, and he stayed awake until he had finished his model. He worked hard all night. When the other animals were fast asleep he threw water on the lumps of earth, and so spoiled the models of the other animals. But in the morning he finished his own, and gave it life long before the others could finish theirs. Thus man was made by Coyote.

THE FIRST MAN AND WOMAN

Nishinam (near Bear River, Cal.)

THE first man created by Coyote was called Aikut. His wife was Yototowi. But the woman grew sick and died. Aikut dug a grave for her close beside his camp fire, for the Nishinam did not burn their dead then. All the light was gone from his life. He wanted to die, so that he could follow Yototowi, and he fell into a deep sleep.

There was a rumbling sound and the spirit of Yototowi arose from the earth and stood beside him. He would have spoken to her, but she forbade him, for when an Indian speaks to a ghost he dies. Then she turned away and set out for the dance-house of ghosts. Aikut followed her. Together they journeyed through a great, dark country, until they came to a river which separated them from the Ghost-land. Over the river there was a bridge of but one small rope, so small that hardly Spider could crawl across it. Here the woman started off alone, but when Aikut stretched out his arms, she returned. Then she started again over the bridge of thread. And Aikut spoke to her, so that he died. Thus together they journeyed to the Spirit-land.

OLD MAN ABOVE AND THE GRIZZLIES

Shastika (*Cal.*)

A LONG time ago, while smoke still curled from the smoke hole of the tepee, a great storm arose. The storm shook the tepee. Wind blew the smoke down the smoke hole. Old Man Above said to Little Daughter: "Climb up to the smoke hole. Tell Wind to be quiet. Stick your arm out of the smoke hole before you tell him." Little Daughter climbed up to the smoke hole and put out her arm. But Little Daughter put out her head also. She wanted to see the world. Little Daughter wanted to see the rivers and trees, and the white foam on the Bitter Waters. Wind caught Little Daughter by the hair. Wind pulled her out of the smoke hole and blew her down the mountain. Wind blew Little Daughter over the smooth ice and the great forests, down to the land of the Grizzlies. Wind tangled her hair and then left her cold and shivering near the tepees of the Grizzlies.

Soon Grizzly came home. In those days Grizzly walked on two feet, and carried a big stick. Grizzly could talk as people do. Grizzly laid down the young elk he had killed and picked up Little Daughter. He took Little Daughter to his tepee. Then Mother Grizzly warmed her by the fire. Mother Grizzly gave her food to eat.

Soon Little Daughter married the son of Grizzly. Their children were not Grizzlies. They were men. So the Grizzlies built a tepee for Little Daughter and her children. White men call the tepee Little Shasta.

At last Mother Grizzly sent a son to Old Man Above. Mother Grizzly knew that Little Daughter was the child of Old Man Above, but she was afraid. She said: "Tell Old Man Above that Little Daughter is alive."

Old Man Above climbed out of the smoke hole. He ran down the mountain side to the land of the Grizzlies. Old Man Above ran very quickly. Wherever he set his foot the snow melted. The snow melted very quickly and made streams of water. Now Grizzlies stood in line to welcome Old Man Above. They stood on two feet and carried clubs. Then Old Man Above saw his daughter and her children. He saw the new race of men. Then Old Man Above became very angry. He said to Grizzlies:

"Never speak again. Be silent. Neither shall ye stand upright. Ye shall use your hands as feet. Ye shall look downward."

Then Old Man Above put out the fire in the tepee. Smoke no longer curls from the smoke hole. He fastened the door of the tepee. The new race of men he drove out. Then Old Man Above took Little Daughter back to his tepee.

That is why grizzlies walk on four feet and look downward. Only when fighting they stand on two feet and use their fists like men.

THE CREATION OF MAN-KIND AND THE FLOOD

Pima (Arizona)

AFTER the world was ready, Earth Doctor made all kinds of animals and creeping things. Then he made images of clay, and told them to be people. After a while there were so many people that there was not food and water enough for all. They were never sick and none died. At last there grew to be so many they were obliged to eat each other. Then Earth Doctor, because he could not give them food and water enough, killed them all. He caught the hook of his staff into the sky and pulled it down so that it crushed all the people and all the animals, until there was nothing living on the earth. Earth Doctor made a hole through the earth with his stick, and through that he went, coming out safe, but alone, on the other side.

He called upon the sun and moon to come out of the wreck of the world and sky, and they did so. But there was no sky for them to travel through, no stars, and no Milky Way. So Earth Doctor made these all

Department of Botanical Research of the Carnegie Institution of Washington

HUTS OF PAPAGO (PIMA) INDIANS, SHOWING VILLAGE BAKE-OVEN

over again. Then he created another race of men and animals.

Then Coyote was born. Moon was his mother. When Coyote was large and strong he came to the land where the Pima Indians lived.

Then Elder Brother was born. Earth was his mother, and Sky his father. He was so powerful that he spoke roughly to Earth Doctor, who trembled before him. The people began to increase in numbers, just as they had done before, but Elder Brother shortened their lives, so the earth did not become so crowded. But Elder Brother did not like the people created by Earth Doctor, so he planned to destroy them again. So Elder Brother planned to create a magic baby. . . .

The screams of the baby shook the earth. They could be heard for a great distance. Then Earth Doctor called all the people together, and told them there would be a great flood. He sang a magic song and then bored a hole through the flat earth-plain through to the other side. Some of the people went into the hole to escape the flood that was coming, but not very many got through. Some of the people asked Elder Brother to help them, but he did not answer. Only Coyote he answered. He told Coyote to find a big log and sit on it, so that he would float on the surface of the water with the driftwood. Elder Brother got into a big olla which he had made, and closed it tight. So he rolled along on the ground under the olla. He sang a magic song as he climbed into his olla.

A young man went to the place where the baby was screaming. Its tears were a great torrent which cut gorges in the earth before it. The water was rising all over the earth. He bent over the child to pick it up, and immediately both became birds and flew above the flood. Only five birds were saved from the flood. One was a flicker and one a vulture. They clung by their beaks to the sky to keep themselves above the waters, but the tail of the flicker was washed by the waves and that is why it is stiff to this day. At last a god took pity on them and gave them power to make "nests of down" from their own breasts on which they floated on the water. One of these birds was the vipisimal, and if any one injures it to this day, the flood may come again.

Now South Doctor called his people to him and told them that a flood was coming. He sang a magic song and he bored a hole in the ground with a cane so that people might go through to the other side. Others he sent to Earth Doctor, but Earth Doctor told them they were too late. So they sent the people to the top of a high mountain called Crooked Mountain. South Doctor sang a magic song and traced his cane around the mountain, but that held back the waters only for a short time. Four times he sang and traced a line around the mountain, yet the flood rose again each time. There was only one thing more to do.

He held his magic crystals in his left hand and sang a song. Then he struck it with his cane. A thunder peal rang through the mountains. He threw his staff into the water and it cracked with a loud noise. Turning, he saw a dog near him. He said, "How high is the tide?" The dog said, "It is very near the top." He looked at the people as he said it. When they heard his voice they all turned to stone. They stood just as they were, and they are there to this day in groups: some of the men talking, some of the women cooking, and some crying.

But Earth Doctor escaped by enclosing himself in his reed staff, which floated upon the water. Elder Brother rolled along in his olla until he came near the mouth of the Colorado River. The olla is now called Black Mountain. After the flood he came out and visited all parts of the land.

When he met Coyote and Earth Doctor, each claimed to have been the first to appear after the flood, but at last they admitted Elder Brother was the first, so he became ruler of the world.

THE BIRDS AND THE FLOOD

Pima (*Arizona*)

ONCE upon a time, when all the earth was flooded, two birds were hanging above the water. They were clinging to the sky with their beaks. The larger bird was gray with a long tail and beak, but the smaller one was the tiny bird that builds a nest shaped like an olla, with only a very small opening at the top. The birds were tired and frightened. The larger one cried and cried, but the little bird held on tight and said, " Don't cry. I 'm littler than you are, but I 'm very brave."

Putnam & Valentine

GRAND CAÑON OF THE COLORADO

Department of Botanical Research of the Carnegie Institution of Washington

THE SANDS OF THE DESERT

LEGEND OF THE FLOOD

Ashochimi (Coast Indians, Cal.)

LONG ago there was a great flood which destroyed all the people in the world. Only Coyote was saved. When the waters subsided, the earth was empty. Coyote thought about it a long time.

Then Coyote collected a great bundle of tail feathers from owls, hawks, eagles, and buzzards. He journeyed over the whole earth and carefully located the site of each Indian village. Where the tepees had stood, he planted a feather in the ground and scraped up the dirt around it. The feathers sprouted like trees, and grew up and branched. At last they turned into men and women. So the world was inhabited with people again.

THE GREAT FLOOD

Sia (New Mexico)

FOR a long time after the fight, the people were very happy, but the ninth year was very bad. The whole earth was filled with water. The water did not fall in rain, but came in as rivers between the mesas. It continued to flow in from all sides until the people and the animals fled to the mesa tops. The water continued to rise until nearly level with the tops of the mesas. Then Sussistinnako cried, "Where shall my people go? Where is the road to the north?" He looked to the north. "Where is the road to the west? Where is the road to the east? Where is the road to the south?" He looked in each direction. He said, "I see the waters are everywhere."

All of the medicine men sang four days and four nights, but still the waters continued to rise.

Then Spider placed a huge reed upon the top of the mesa. He said, "My people will pass up through this to the world above."

Utset led the way, carrying a sack in which were many of the Star people. The medicine men followed, carrying sacred things in sacred blankets on their backs. Then came the people, and the animals, and the snakes, and birds. The turkey was far behind and the foam of the water rose and reached the tip ends of his feathers. You may know that is true because even to this day they bear the mark of the waters.

When they reached the top of the great reed, the earth which formed the floor of the world above, barred their way. Utset called to Locust, " Man, come here." Locust went to her. She said, " You know best how to pass through the earth. Go and make a door for us."

" Very well, mother," said Locust. " I think I can make a way."

He began working with his feet and after a while he passed through the earthy floor, entering the upper world. As soon as he saw it, he said to Utset, " It is good above."

Utset called Badger, and said, " Make a door for us. Sika, the Locust has made one, but it is very small."

" Very well, mother, I will," said Badger.

After much work he passed into the world above, and said,

" Mother, I have opened the way." Badger also said, " Father-mother, the world above is good."

Utset then called Deer. She said, " You go through

first. If you can get your head through, others may pass."

The deer returned saying, "Father, it is all right. I passed without trouble."

Utset called Elk. She said, "You pass through. If you can get your head and horns through the door, all may pass."

Elk returned saying, "Father, it is good. I passed without trouble."

Then Utset told the buffalo to try, and he returned saying, "Father-mother, the door is good. I passed without trouble."

Utset called the scarab beetle and gave him the sack of stars, telling him to pass out first with them. Scarab did not know what the sack contained, but he was very small and grew tired carrying it. He wondered what could be in the sack. After entering the new world he was so tired he laid down the sack and peeped into it. He cut only a tiny hole, but at once the Star People flew out and filled the heavens everywhere.

Then Utset and all the people came, and after Turkey passed, the door was closed with a great rock so that the waters from below could not follow them.

Then Utset looked for the sack with the Star People. She found it nearly empty and could not tell where the stars had gone. The little beetle sat by, very much frightened and very sad. But Utset was angry and said, "You are bad and disobedient. From this time forth, you shall be blind." That is the reason the scarabæus has no eyes, so the old ones say.

But the little fellow had saved a few of the stars by grasping the sack and holding it fast. Utset placed these in the heavens. In one group she placed seven — the great bear. In another, three. In another group she placed the Pleiades, and threw the others far off into the sky.

THE FLOOD AND THE THEFT OF FIRE

Tolowa (Del Norte Co., Cal.)

A LONG time ago there came a great rain. It lasted a long time and the water kept rising till all the valleys were submerged, and the Indian tribes fled to the high lands. But the water rose, and though the Indians fled to the highest point, all were swept away and drowned — all but one man and one woman. They reached the very highest peak and were saved. These two Indians ate the fish from the waters around them.

Then the waters subsided. All the game was gone, and all the animals. But the children of these two Indians, when they died, became the spirits of deer and bear and insects, and so the animals and insects came back to the earth again.

The Indians had no fire. The flood had put out all the fires in the world. They looked at the moon and wished they could secure fire from it. Then the Spider Indians and the Snake Indians formed a plan to steal fire. The Spiders wove a very light balloon, and fastened it by a long rope to the earth. Then they climbed into the balloon and started for the moon. But the Indians of the Moon were suspicious of the Earth Indians. The Spiders said, "We came to gamble." The Moon Indians were much pleased and all the Spider Indians began to gamble with them. They sat by the fire.

Then the Snake Indians sent a man to climb up the long rope from the earth to the moon. He climbed the rope, and darted through the fire before the Moon Indians understood what he had done. Then he slid down the rope to earth again. As soon as he touched the earth he travelled over the rocks, the trees, and the dry sticks lying upon the ground, giving fire to each. Everything he touched contained fire. So the world became bright again, as it was before the flood.

When the Spider Indians came down to earth again, they were immediately put to death, for the tribes were afraid the Moon Indians might want revenge.

LEGEND OF THE FLOOD IN SACRAMENTO VALLEY

Maidu (near Sacramento Valley, Cal.)

LONG, long ago the Indians living in Sacramento Valley were happy. Suddenly there came the swift sound of rushing waters, and the valley became like Big Waters, which no man can measure. The Indians fled, but many slept beneath the waves. Also the frogs and the salmon pursued them and they ate many Indians. Only two who fled into the foothills escaped. To these two, Great Man gave many children, and many tribes arose. But one great chief ruled all the nation. The chief went out upon a wide knoll overlooking Big Waters, and he knew that the plains of his people were beneath the waves. Nine sleeps he lay on the knoll, thinking thoughts of these great waters. Nine sleeps he lay without food, and his mind was thinking always of one thing: How did this deep water cover the plains of the world?

At the end of nine sleeps he was changed. He was not like himself. No arrow could wound him. He was like Great Man for no Indian could slay him. Then

Putnam & Valentine

". . . so that the waters on the plains flower into big Waters"
(Golden Gate)

Putnam & Valentine

FALLEN LEAF LAKE

he spoke to Great Man and commanded him to banish the waters from the plains of his ancestors. Great Man tore a hole in the mountain side, so that the waters on the plains flowed into Big Waters. Thus the Sacramento River was formed.

THE FABLE OF THE ANIMALS

Karok (near Klamath River, Cal.)

A GREAT many hundred snows ago, Kareya, sitting on the Sacred Stool, created the world. First, he made the fishes in the Big Water, then the animals on the green land, and last of all, Man! But at first the animals were all alike in power. No one knew which animals should be food for others, and which should be food for man. Then Kareya ordered them all to meet in one place, that Man might give each his rank and his power. So the animals all met together one evening, when the sun was set, to wait overnight for the coming of Man on the next morning. Kareya also commanded Man to make bows and arrows, as many as there were animals, and to give the longest one to the animal which was to have the most power, and the shortest to the one which should have least power. So he did, and after nine sleeps his work was ended, and the bows and arrows which he had made were very many.

Now the animals, being all together, went to sleep, so they might be ready to meet Man on the next morning. But Coyote was exceedingly cunning — he was cunning above all the beasts. Coyote wanted the longest bow and the greatest power, so he could have all the other animals for his meat. He decided to stay awake all night, so that he would be first to meet Man in the morning. So he laughed to himself and stretched his nose out on his paw and pretended to sleep. About midnight he began to be sleepy. He had to walk around the camp and scratch his eyes to keep them open. He grew more sleepy, so that he had to skip and jump about to keep awake. But he made so much noise, he awakened some of the other animals. When the morning star came up, he was too sleepy to keep his eyes open any longer. So he took two little sticks, and sharpened them at the ends, and propped open his eyelids. Then he felt safe. He watched the morning star, with his nose stretched along his paws, and fell asleep. The sharp sticks pinned his eyelids fast together.

The morning star rose rapidly into the sky. The birds began to sing. The animals woke up and stretched themselves, but still Coyote lay fast asleep. When the sun rose, the animals went to meet Man. He gave the longest bow to Cougar, so he had greatest power; the second longest he gave to Bear; others he gave to the other animals, giving all but the last to

Frog. But the shortest one was left. Man cried out, "What animal have I missed?" Then the animals began to look about and found Coyote fast asleep, with his eyelids pinned together. All the animals began to laugh, and they jumped upon Coyote and danced upon him. Then they led him to Man, still blinded, and Man pulled out the sharp sticks and gave him the shortest bow of all. It would hardly shoot an arrow farther than a foot. All the animals laughed.

But Man took pity on Coyote, because he was now weaker even than Frog. So at his request, Kareya gave him cunning, ten times more than before, so that he was cunning above all the animals of the wood. Therefore Coyote was friendly to Man and his children, and did many things for them.

Putnam & Valentine

San Luis Rey Mission

COYOTE AND SUN

Pai Ute (near Kern River, Cal.)

A LONG time ago, Coyote wanted to go to the sun. He asked Pokoh, Old Man, to show him the trail. Coyote went straight out on this trail and he travelled it all day. But Sun went round so that Coyote came back at night to the place from which he started in the morning.

The next morning, Coyote asked Pokoh to show him the trail. Pokoh showed him, and Coyote travelled all day and came back at night to the same place again.

But the third day, Coyote started early and went out on the trail to the edge of the world and sat down on the hole where the sun came up. While waiting for the sun he pointed with his bow and arrow at different places and pretended to shoot. He also pretended not to see the sun. When Sun came up, he told Coyote to get out of his way. Coyote told him to go around; that it was his trail. But Sun came up under him and he had to hitch forward a little. After Sun came up a little farther, it began to get hot on Coyote's shoulder, so he spit on his paw and rubbed his shoulder. Then he wanted to ride up with the sun. Sun said, "Oh, no"; but Coyote insisted. So Coyote climbed up on Sun, and Sun started up the trail in the sky. The trail was marked off into steps like a ladder. As Sun went up he counted "one, two, three," and so on. By and by Coyote became very thirsty, and he asked Sun for a drink of water. Sun gave him an acorn-cup full. Coyote asked him why he had no more. About noon-time, Coyote became very impatient. It was very hot. Sun told him to shut his eyes. Coyote shut them, but opened them again. He kept opening and shutting them all the afternoon. At night, when Sun came down, Coyote took hold of a tree. Then he clambered off Sun and climbed down to the earth.

THE COURSE OF THE SUN

Sia (New Mexico)

SUSSISTINNAKO, the spider, said to the sun, " My son, you will ascend and pass over the world above. You will go from north to south. Return and tell me what you think of it."

The sun said, on his return, " Mother, I did as you bade me, and I did not like the road."

Spider told him to ascend and pass over the world from west to the east. On his return, the sun said,

" It may be good for some, mother, but I did not like it."

Spider said, " You will again ascend and pass over the straight road from the east to the west. Return and tell me what you think of it."

That night the sun said, " I am much contented. I like that road much."

Sussistinnako said, " My son, you will ascend each day and pass over the world from east to west."

Upon each day's journey the sun stops midway from the east to the centre of the world to eat his breakfast.

In the centre he stops to eat his dinner. Halfway from the centre to the west he stops to eat his supper. He never fails to eat these three meals each day, and always stops at the same points.

The sun wears a shirt of dressed deerskin, with leggings of the same reaching to his thighs. The shirt and leggings are fringed. His moccasins are also of deerskin and embroidered in yellow, red, and turkis beads. He wears a kilt of deerskin, having a snake painted upon it. He carries a bow and arrows, the quiver being of cougar skin, hanging over his shoulder, and he holds his bow in his left hand and an arrow in his right. He always wears the mask which protects him from the sight of the people of Ha-arts.

At the top of the mask is an eagle plume with parrot plumes; an eagle plume is at each side, and one at the bottom of the mask. The hair around the head and face is red like fire, and when it moves and shakes people cannot look closely at the mask. It is not intended that they should observe closely, else they would know that instead of seeing the sun they see only his mask.

The moon came to the upper world with the sun and he also wears a mask.

Each night the sun passes by the house of Sussistinnako, the spider, who asks him, "How are my children above? How many have died to-day? How many have been born to-day?" The sun lingers only long enough to answer his questions. He then passes on to his house in the east.

THE FOXES AND THE SUN

Yurok (near Klamath River, Cal.)

ONCE upon a time, the Foxes were angry with Sun. They held a council about the matter. Then twelve Foxes were selected — twelve of the bravest to catch Sun and tie him down. They made ropes of sinew; then the twelve watched until the Sun, as he followed the downward trail in the sky, touched the top of a certain hill. Then the Foxes caught Sun, and tied him fast to the hill. But the Indians saw them, and they killed the Foxes with arrows. Then they cut the sinews. But the Sun had burned a great hole in the ground. The Indians know the story is true, because they can see the hole which Sun burned.

THE THEFT OF FIRE

Karok (near Klamath River, Cal.)

THERE was no fire on earth and the Karoks were cold and miserable. Far away to the east, hidden in a treasure box, was fire which Kareya had made and given to two old hags, lest the Karoks should steal it. So Coyote decided to steal fire for the Indians.

Coyote called a great council of the animals. After the council he stationed a line from the land of the Karoks to the distant land where the fire was kept. Lion was nearest the Fire Land, and Frog was nearest the Karok land. Lion was strongest and Frog was weakest, and the other animals took their places, according to the power given them by Man.

Then Coyote took an Indian with him and went to the hill top, but he hid the Indian under the hill. Coyote went to the tepee of the hags. He said, "Good-evening." They replied, "Good-evening."

Coyote said, "It is cold out here. Can you let me sit by the fire?" So they let him sit by the fire. He was only a coyote. He stretched his nose out along his forepaws and pretended to go to sleep, but he kept the corner of one eye open watching. So he spent all night watching and thinking, but he had no chance to get a piece of the fire.

The next morning Coyote held a council with the Indian. He told him when he, Coyote, was within the tepee, to attack it. Then Coyote went back to the fire. The hags let him in again. He was only a coyote. But Coyote stood close by the casket of fire. The Indian made a dash at the tepee. The hags rushed out after him, and Coyote seized a fire brand in his teeth and flew over the ground. The hags saw the sparks flying and gave chase. But Coyote reached Lion, who ran with it to Grizzly Bear. Grizzly Bear ran with it to Cinnamon Bear; he ran with it to Wolf, and at last the fire came to Ground-Squirrel. Squirrel took the brand and ran so fast that his tail caught fire. He curled it up over his back, and burned the black spot in his shoulders. You can see it even to-day. Squirrel came to Frog, but Frog could n't run. He opened his mouth wide and swallowed the fire. Then he jumped but the hags caught his tail. Frog jumped again, but the hags kept his tail. That is why Frogs have no tail, even to this day. Frog swam under water, and came up on a pile of driftwood. He spat out the fire into the dry wood, and that is why there is fire in dry wood even to-day. When an Indian rubs two pieces together, the fire comes out.

THE THEFT OF FIRE

Sia (New Mexico)

A LONG, long time ago, the people became tired of feeding on grass, like deer and wild animals, and they talked together how fire might be found. The Ti-amoni said, "Coyote is the best man to steal fire from the world below," so he sent for Coyote.

When Coyote came, the Ti-amoni said, "The people wish for fire. We are tired of feeding on grass. You must go to the world below and bring the fire."

Coyote said, "It is well, father. I will go."

So Coyote slipped stealthily to the house of Sussistinnako. It was the middle of the night. Snake, who guarded the first door, was asleep, and he slipped quickly and quietly by. Cougar, who guarded the second door, was asleep, and Coyote slipped by. Bear, who guarded the third door, was also sleeping. At the fourth door, Coyote found the guardian of the fire asleep. Slipping through into the room of Sussistinnako he found him also sleeping.

Coyote quickly lighted the cedar brand which was

attached to his tail and hurried out. Spider awoke, just enough to know some one was leaving the room. "Who is there?" he cried. Then he called, "Some one has been here." But before he could waken the sleeping Bear and Cougar and Snake, Coyote had almost reached the upper world.

Courtesy of Smithsonian Institution

SIA CEREMONIAL VASE

THE EARTH-HARDENING AFTER THE FLOOD

Sia (New Mexico)

AFTER the flood, the Sia returned to Ha-arts, the earth. They came through an opening in the far north. After they had remained at their first village a year, they wished to pass on, but the earth was very moist and Utset was puzzled how to harden it.

Utset called Cougar. She said, " Have you any medicine to harden the road so that we may pass over it? " Cougar replied, " I will try, mother." But after going a short distance over the road, he sank to his shoulders in the wet earth. He returned much afraid and told Utset that he could go no farther.

Then she sent for Bear. She said, " Have you any medicine to harden the road? " Bear started out, but he sank to his shoulders, and returned saying, " I can do nothing."

Then Utset called Badger, and he tried. She called Shrew, and he failed. She called Wolf, and he failed.

Then Utset returned to the lower world and asked

Sussistinnako what she could do to harden the earth so that her people might travel over it. He asked, "Have you no medicine to make the earth firm? Have you asked Cougar and Wolf, Bear and Badger and Wolf to use their medicines to harden the earth?"

Utset said, "I have tried all these."

Then Sussistinnako said, "Others will understand." He told her to have a woman of the Kapina (spider) clan try to harden the earth.

When the woman arrived, Utset said, "My mother, Sussistinnako tells me the Kapina society understand how to harden the earth."

The woman said, "I do not know how to make the earth hard."

Three times Utset asked the woman about hardening the earth, and three times the woman said, "I do not know." The fourth time the woman said, "Well, I guess I know. I will try."

So she called together the members of the Spider society, the Kapina, and said,

"Our mother, Sussistinnako, bids us work for her and harden the earth so that the people may pass over it." The spider woman first made a road of fine cotton which she produced from her own body, and suspended it a few feet above the earth. Then she told the people they could travel on that. But the people were afraid to trust themselves to such a frail road.

Then Utset said, "I wish a man and not a woman of the Spider society to work for me."

Then he came. He threw out a charm of wood, latticed so it could be expanded or contracted. When it was extended it reached to the middle of the earth. He threw it to the south, to the east, and to the west; then he threw it toward the people in the north.

So the earth was made firm that the people might travel upon it.

Soon after Utset said, "I will soon leave you. I will return to the home from which I came."

Then she selected a man of the Corn clan. She said to him, "You will be known as Ti-amoni (arch-ruler). You will be to my people as myself. You will pass with them over the straight road. I give to you all my wisdom, my thoughts, my heart, and all. I fill your mind with my mind."

He replied: "It is well, mother. I will do as you say."

THE ORIGINS OF THE TOTEMS AND OF NAMES

Zuni (New Mexico)

NOW the Twain Beloved and the priest-fathers gathered in council for the naming and selection of man-groups and creature-kinds, and things. So they called the people of the southern space the Children of Summer, and those who loved the sun most became the Sun people. Others who loved the water became the Toad people, or Turtle people, or Frog people. Others loved the seeds of the earth and became the Seed people, or the people of the First-growing grass, or of the Tobacco. Those who loved warmth were the Fire or Badger people. According to their natures they chose their totems.

And so also did the People of Winter, or the People of the North. Some were known as the Bear people, or the Coyote people, or Deer people; others as the Crane people, Turkey people, or Grouse people. So the Badger people dwelt in a warm place, even as the badgers on the sunny side of hills burrow, finding a dwelling amongst the dry roots whence is fire.

TRADITIONS OF WANDERINGS

Hopi (Arizona)

AFTER the Hopi had been taught to build stone houses, they took separate ways. My people were the Snake people. They lived in snake skins, each family occupying a separate snake skin bag. All were hung on the end of a rainbow which swung around until the end touched Navajo Mountain. Then the bags dropped from it. Wherever a bag dropped, there was their house. After they arranged their bags they came out from them as men and women, and they then built a stone house which had five sides. Then a brilliant star arose in the southeast. It would shine for a while and disappear.

The old men said, "Beneath that star there must be people." They decided to travel to it. They cut a staff and set it in the ground and watched until the star reached its top. Then they started and travelled as long as the star shone. When it disappeared they halted. But the star did not shine every night. Sometimes many years passed before it appeared again.

When this occurred, the people built houses during their halt. They built round houses and square houses, and all the ruins between here and Navajo Mountain mark the places where our people lived. They waited until the star came to the top of the staff again, but when they moved on, many people remained in those houses.

When our people reached Waipho (a spring a few miles from Walpi) the star vanished. It has never been seen since. They built a house there, but Masauwu, the God of the Face of the Earth, came and compelled the people to move about halfway between the East Mesa and the Middle Mesa and there they stayed many plantings. One time when the old men were assembled, the god came among them, looking like a horrible skeleton and rattling his bones. But he could not frighten them. So he said, "I have lost my wager. All that I have is yours. Ask for anything you want and I will give it to you."

At that time, our people's house was beside the water course. The god said, "Why do you sit there in the mud? Go up yonder where it is dry."

So they went across to the west side of the mesa near the point and built a house and lived there.

Again when the old men assembled two demons

Putnam & Valentine

FROM THE BELL-TOWER OF SAN XAVIER MISSION, TUCSON, ARIZONA

Putnam & Valentine

INDIANS IN THE GRAND CAÑON

came among them, but the old men took the great Baho and chased them away.

Other Hopi (Hopituh) came into this country from time to time and old people said, "Build here," or "Build there," and portioned the land among the newcomers.

THE MIGRATION OF THE WATER PEOPLE

Walpi (Arizona)

IN the long ago, the Snake, Horn, and Eagle people lived here (in Tusayan) but their corn grew only a span high and when they sang for rain, the Cloud god sent only a thin mist. My people lived then in the distant Pa-lat Kwa-bi in the South. There was a very bad old man there. When he met any one he would spit in their faces. . . . He did all manner of evil. Baholihonga got angry at this and turned the world upside down. Water spouted up through the kivas and through the fire places in the houses. The earth was rent in great chasms, and water covered everything except one narrow ridge of mud. Across this the Serpent-god told all the people to travel. As they journeyed across, the feet of the bad slipped and they fell into the dark water. The good people, after many days, reached dry land.

While the water was rising around the village, the old people got on top of the houses. They thought they could not struggle across with the younger people. But Baholihonga clothed them with the skins of turkeys. They spread their wings out and floated in the air just above the surface of the water, and in this way they got across. There were saved of us, the Water people, the Corn people, the Lizard, Horned-toad, and Sand peoples, two families of Rabbit, and the Tobacco people. The turkey tail dragged in the water. That is why there is white on the turkey's tail now. This is also the reason why old people use turkey-feathers at the religious ceremonies.

COYOTE AND THE MESQUITE BEANS

Pima (*Arizona*)

AFTER the waters of the flood had gone down, Elder Brother said to Coyote, "Do not touch that black bug; and do not eat the mesquite beans. It is dangerous to harm anything that came safe through the flood."

So Coyote went on, but presently he came to the black bug. He stopped and ate it up. Then he went on to the mesquite beans. He stopped and looked at them a while, and then said, "I will just taste one and that will be all." But he stood there and ate and ate until he had eaten them all up. And the bug and the beans swelled up in his stomach and killed him.

ORIGIN OF THE SIERRA NEVADAS AND COAST RANGE

Yokuts (near Fresno, Cal.)

ONCE there was a time when there was nothing in the world but water. About the place where Tulare Lake is now, there was a pole standing far up out of the water, and on this pole perched Hawk and Crow. First Hawk would sit on the pole a while, then Crow would knock him off and sit on it himself. Thus they sat on the top of the pole above the water for many ages. At last they created the birds which prey on fish. They created Kingfisher, Eagle, Pelican, and others. They created also Duck. Duck was very small but she dived to the bottom of the water, took a beakful of mud, and then died in coming to the top of the water. Duck lay dead floating on the water. Then Hawk and Crow took the mud from Duck's beak, and began making the mountains.

They began at the place now known as Ta-hi-cha-pa Pass, and Hawk made the east range. Crow made the west one. They pushed the mud down hard into the water and then piled it high. They worked toward the north. At last Hawk and Crow met at Mount Shasta. Then their work was done. But when they looked at their mountains, Crow's range was much larger than Hawk's.

Hawk said to Crow, "How did this happen, you rascal? You have been stealing earth from my bill. That is why your mountains are the biggest." Crow laughed.

Then Hawk chewed some Indian tobacco. That made him wise. At once he took hold of the mountains and turned them around almost in a circle. He put his range where Crow's had been. That is why the Sierra Nevada Range is larger than the Coast Range.

Putnam & Valentine

Happy Isles, Yosemite

Putnam & Valentine

A-WAI'-A (MIRROR LAKE)

YOSEMITE VALLEY

(*Explanatory*) [1]

MR. STEPHEN POWERS claims that there is no such word in the Miwok language as *Yosemite*.

" The valley has always been known to them, and is to this day, when speaking among themselves, as *A-wa'-ni*. This, it is true, is only the name of one of the ancient villages which it contained; but by prominence it gave its name to the valley, and in accordance with Indian usage almost everywhere, to the inhabitants of the same. The word *Yosemite* is simply a very beautiful and sonorous corruption of the word for grizzly bear. On the Stanislaus and north of it, the word is *u-zu'-mai-ti;* at Little Gap, *o-so'-mai-ti;* in Yosemite itself, *u-zu'-mai-ti;* on the South Fork of the Merced, *uh-zu'-mai-tuh*. . . .

"In the following list, the signification of the name is given whenever there is any known to the Indians:

[1] The explanation given above is that made by Mr. Stephen Powers, in Vol. 3, U. S. Geographical and Geological Survey of the Rocky Mountain region, Part 2, Contributions to North American Ethnology, 1877.

"Wa-kal′-la (the river), Merced River.

"Lung-u-tu-ku′-ya, Ribbon Fall.

"Po′-ho-no, Po-ho′-no (though the first is probably the more correct), Bridal-Veil Fall. . . . This word is said to signify 'evil wind.' The only 'evil wind' that an Indian knows of is a whirlwind, which is *poi-i′-cha* or *Kan′-u-ma.*

"Tu-tok-a-nu′-la, El Capitan. 'Measuring-worm stone.' [Legend is given elsewhere.]

"Ko-su′-ko, Cathedral Rock.

"Pu-si′-na, and Chuk′-ka (the squirrel and the acorn-cache), a tall, sharp needle, with a smaller one at its base, just east of Cathedral Rock. . . . The savages . . . imagined here a squirrel nibbling at the base of an acorn granary.

"Loi′-a, Sentinel Rock.

"Sak′-ka-du-eh, Sentinel Dome.

"Cho′-lok (the fall), Yosemite Fall. This is the generic word for 'fall.'

"Ma′-ta (the cañon), Indian Cañon. A generic word, in explaining which the Indians hold up both hands to denote perpendicular walls.

"Ham′-mo-ko (usually contracted to Ham′-moak), . . . broken debris lying at the foot of the walls.

"U-zu′-mai-ti La′-wa-tuh (grizzly bear skin), Glacier Rock . . . from the grayish, grizzled appearance of the wall.

Putnam & Valentine

Po′-ho-no (Bridal Veil Falls)

Putnam & Valentine

CHOLOK, "THE FALL"

"Cho-ko-nip′-o-deh (baby-basket), Royal Arches. This . . . canopy-rock bears no little resemblance to an Indian baby-basket. Another form is *cho-ko′-ni,* . . . literally . . . 'dog-house.'

"Pai-wai′-ak (white water?), Vernal Fall.

"Yo-wai-yi, Nevada Fall. In this word is detected the root of *Awaia,* 'a lake' or body of water.

"Tis-se′-yak, South Dome. [See legend elsewhere.]

"To-ko′-ye, North Dome, husband of Tisseyak. [See legend elsewhere.]

"Shun′-ta, Hun′-ta (the eye), Watching Eye.

"A-wai′-a (a lake), Mirror Lake.

"Sa-wah′ (a gap), a name occurring frequently.

"Wa-ha′-ka, a village which stood at the base of Three Brothers; also the rock itself. This was the westernmost village in the valley.

"There were nine villages in Yosemite Valley and . . . formerly others extending as far down as the Bridal Veil Fall, which were destroyed in wars that occurred before the whites came."

LEGEND OF TU-TOK-A-NU'-LA (EL CAPITAN)

Yosemite Valley

THERE were once two little boys living in the valley who went down to the river to swim. After paddling and splashing about to their hearts' content, they went on shore and crept up on a huge boulder which stood beside the water. They lay down in the warm sunshine to dry themselves, but fell asleep. They slept so soundly that they knew nothing, though the great boulder grew day by day, and rose night by night, until it lifted them up beyond the sight of their tribe, who looked for them everywhere.

The rock grew until the boys were lifted high into the heaven, even far up above the blue sky, until they scraped their faces against the moon. And still, year after year, among the clouds they slept.

Then there was held a great council of all the animals to bring the boys down from the top of the great rock. Every animal leaped as high as he could up the face of the rocky wall. Mouse could only jump as high as one's hand; Rat, twice as high. Then Raccoon

Putnam & Valentine

" THEN CAME THE TINY MEASURING WORM AND BEGAN TO CREEP UP THE ROCK " (EL CAPITAN)

Putnam & Valentine

Cathedral Spires

tried; he could jump a little farther. One after another of the animals tried, and Grizzly Bear made a great leap far up the wall, but fell back. Last of all Lion tried, and he jumped farther than any other animal, but fell down upon his back. Then came tiny Measuring-Worm, and began to creep up the rock. Soon he reached as high as Raccoon had jumped, then as high as Bear, then as high as Lion's leap, and by and by he was out of sight, climbing up the face of the rock. For one whole snow, Measuring-Worm climbed the rock, and at last he reached the top. Then he wakened the boys, and came down the same way he went up, and brought them down safely to the ground. Therefore the rock is called Tutokanula, the measuring worm. But white men call it El Capitan.

LEGEND OF TIS-SE′-YAK (SOUTH DOME AND NORTH DOME)

Yosemite Valley

TISSEYAK and her husband journeyed from a country very far off, and entered the valley of the Yosemite foot-sore from travel. She bore a great heavy conical basket, strapped across her head. Tisseyak came first. Her husband followed with a rude staff and a light roll of skins on his back. They were thirsty after their long journey across the mountains. They hurried forward to drink of the waters, and the woman was still in advance when she reached Lake Awaia. Then she dipped up the water in her basket and drank of it. She drank up all the water. The lake was dry before her husband reached it. And because the woman drank all the water, there came a drought. The earth dried up. There was no grass, nor any green thing.

But the man was angry because he had no water to drink. He beat the woman with his staff and she fled, but he followed and beat her even more. Then the woman wept. In her anger she turned and flung her

Putnam & Valentine

Yosemite Valley. Vernal Falls and Nevada Falls from Glacier Point

Putnam & Valentine

"South Dome is the woman and North Dome is the husband"

basket at the man. And even then they were changed into stone. The woman's basket lies upturned beside the man. The woman's face is tear-stained, with long dark lines trailing down.

South Dome is the woman and North Dome is the husband. The Indian woman cuts her hair straight across the forehead, and allows the sides to drop along her cheeks, forming a square face.

HISTORIC TRADITION OF THE UPPER TUOLUMNE

Yosemite Valley

(As given by Mr. Stephen Powers, 1877.)[1]

THERE is a lake-like expansion of the Upper Tuolumne some four miles long and from a half mile to a mile wide, directly north of Hatchatchie Valley (erroneously spelled Hetch Hetchy). It appears to have no name among Americans, but the Indians call it O-wai-a-nuh, which is manifestly a dialectic variation of *a-wai'-a,* the generic word for "lake." Nat. Screech, a veteran mountaineer and hunter, states that he visited this region in 1850, and at that time there was a valley along the river having the same dimensions that this lake now has. Again, in 1855, he happened to pass that way and discovered that the lake had been formed as it now exists. He was at a loss to account for its origin; but subsequently he acquired the Miwok language as spoken at Little Gap, and while listening to the Indians one day he

[1] (Vol. 3, Part 2, U. S. Geographical and Geological Survey of the Rocky Mountain region: Contributions to North American Ethnology, 1877.)

overheard them casually refer to the formation of this lake in an extraordinary manner. On being questioned they stated that there had been a tremendous cataclysm in that valley, the bottom of it having fallen out apparently, whereby the entire valley was submerged in the waters of the river. As nearly as he could ascertain from their imperfect methods of reckoning time, this occurred in 1851; and in that year, while in the town of Sonora, Screech and many others remembered to have heard a huge explosion in that direction which they then supposed was caused by a local earthquake.

On Drew's Ranch, Middle Fork of the Tuolumne, lives an aged squaw called Dish-i, who was in the valley when this remarkable event occurred. According to her account the earth dropped in beneath their feet, and waters of the river leaped up and came rushing upon them in a vast, roaring flood, almost perpendicular like a wall of rock. At first the Indians were stricken dumb, and motionless with terror, but when they saw the waters coming, they escaped for life, though thirty or forty were overtaken and drowned. Another squaw named Isabel says that the stubs of trees, which are still plainly visible deep down in the pellucid waters, are considered by the old superstitious Indians to be evil spirits, the demons of the place, reaching up their arms, and that they fear them greatly.

CALIFORNIA BIG TREES

Pai Utes (near Kern River, Cal.)

THE California big trees are sacred to the Monos, who call them "*woh-woh-nau,*" a word formed in imitation of the hoot of the owl. The owl is the guardian spirit and the god of the big trees. Bad luck comes to those who cut down the big trees, or shoot at an owl, or shoot in the presence of the owl.

In old days the Indians tried to persuade the white men not to cut down the big trees. When they see the trees cut down they call after the white men. They say the owl will bring them evil.

Putnam & Valentine

WOH-WOH-NAU, THE SACRED TREES OF THE MONOS

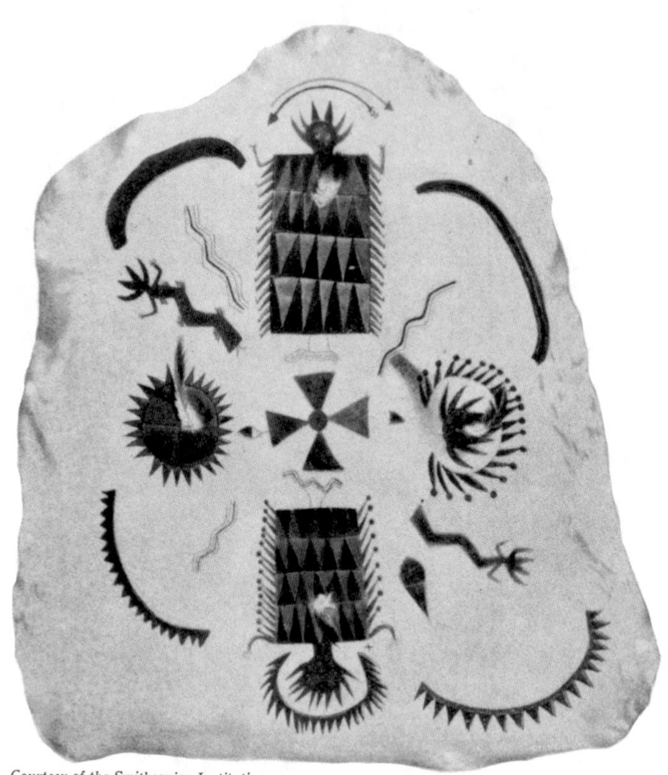

Courtesy of the Smithsonian Institution

APACHE MEDICINE SHIRT

THE CHILDREN OF CLOUD

Pima (Arizona)

WHEN the Hohokam dwelt on the Gila River and tilled their farms around the great temple which we call Casa Grande, there was a beautiful young woman in the pueblo who had two twin sons. Their father was Cloud, and he lived far away.

One day the boys came to their mother, as she was weaving mats. "Who is our father?" they asked. "We have no one to run to when he returns from the hunt, or from war, to shout to him."

The mother answered: "In the morning, look toward the sunrise and you will see a white Cloud standing upright. He is your father."

"Can we visit our father?" they asked.

"Yes," said their mother. "You may visit him, but you must make the journey without stopping. First you will reach Wind, who is your father's eldest brother. Behind him you will find your father."

The boys travelled four days and came to the house of Wind.

"Are you our father?" they asked.

"No, I am your Uncle," answered Wind. "Your father lives in the next house. Go on to him."

They travelled on to Cloud. But Cloud drove them away. He said, "Go to your uncle Wind. He will tell you something." But Wind sent them back to Cloud again. Thus the boys were driven away from each house four times.

Then Cloud said to them, "Prove to me you are my sons. If you are, you can do what I do."

The younger boy sent chain lightning across the sky with sharp, crackling thunder. The elder boy sent the heat lightning with its distant rumble of thunder.

"You are my children," said Cloud. "You have power like mine."

But again he tested them. He took them to a house near by where a flood of rain had drowned the people. "If they are my sons," he said, "they will not be harmed."

Then Cloud sent the rain and the storm. The water rose higher and higher, but the two boys were not harmed. The water could not drown them. Then Cloud took them to his home and there they stayed a long, long time.

But after a long time, the boys wished to see their mother again. Then Cloud made them some bows and arrows differing from any they had ever seen, and sent them to their mother. He told them he would watch over them as they travelled but they must speak to no one they met on their way.

So the boys travelled to the setting sun. First they met Raven. They remembered their father's command and turned aside so as not to meet him. Then they met Roadrunner, and turned aside to avoid him. Next came Hawk and Eagle.

Eagle said, "Let 's scare those boys." So he swooped down over their heads until they cried from fright.

"We were just teasing you," said Eagle. "We will not do you any harm." Then Eagle flew on.

Next they met Coyote. They tried to avoid him, but Coyote ran around and put himself in their way. Cloud was watching and he sent down thunder and lightning. And the boys sent out their magic thunder and lightning also, until Coyote was frightened and ran away.

Now this happened on the mountain top, and one boy was standing on each side of the trail. After Coyote ran away, they were changed into mescal — the very largest mescal ever known. The place was near Tucson. This is the reason why mescal grows on the mountains, and why thunder and lightning go from place to place — because the children did. That is why it rains when we gather mescal.

THE CLOUD PEOPLE

Sia (New Mexico)

NOW all the Cloud People, the Lightning People, the Thunder and Rainbow Peoples followed the Sia into the upper world. But all the people of Tinia, the middle world, did not leave the lower world. Only a portion were sent by the Spider to work for the people of the upper world. The Cloud People are so many that, although the demands of the earth people are so great, there are always many passing about over Tinia for pleasure. These Cloud People ride on wheels, small wheels being used by the little Cloud children and large wheels by the older ones.[1]

The Cloud People keep always behind their masks. The shape of the mask depends upon the number of the people and the work being done. The Henati are the floating white clouds behind which the Cloud People pass for pleasure. The Heash are clouds like the

[1] The Indians say the Americans also ride wheels, therefore they must have known about the Cloud People.

Courtesy of F. Ellerman, Mount Wilson Solar Observatory

"THE HERATI ARE THE FLOATING WHITE CLOUDS . . ."

Courtesy of F. Ellerman, Mount Wilson Solar Observatory

"THE HEASH ARE CLOUDS LIKE THE PLAINS . . ."

plains and behind these the Cloud People are laboring to water the earth. Water is brought by the Cloud People, from the springs at the base of the mountains, in gourds and jugs and vases by the men, women, and children. They rise from the springs and pass through the trunk of the tree to its top, which reaches Tinia. They pass on to the point to be sprinkled.

The priest of the Cloud People is above even the priests of the Thunder, Lightning, and Rainbow Peoples. The Cloud People have ceremonials, just like those of the Sia. On the altars of the Sia may be seen figures arranged just as the Cloud People sit in their ceremonials.

When a priest of the Cloud People wishes assistance from the Thunder and Lightning Peoples, he notifies their priests, but keeps a supervision of all things himself.

Then the Lightning People shoot their arrows to make it rain the harder. The smaller flashes come from the bows of the children. The Thunder People have human forms, with wings of knives, and by flapping these wings they make a great noise. Thus they frighten the Cloud and Lightning People into working the harder.

The Rainbow People were created to work in Tinia to make it more beautiful for the people of Ha-arts, the earth, to look upon. The elders make the beautiful rainbows, but the children assist. The Sia have no idea of what or how these bows are made. They do know, however, that war heroes always travel upon the rainbows.

RAIN SONG

Sia (New Mexico)

WE, the ancient ones, ascended from the middle of the world below, through the door of the entrance to the lower world, we hold our songs to the Cloud, Lightning, and Thunder Peoples as we hold our own hearts. Our medicine is precious.

(Addressing the people of Tinia:)

We entreat you to send your thoughts to us so that we may sing your songs straight, so that they will pass over the straight road to the Cloud priests that they may cover the earth with water, so that she may bear all that is good for us.

Lightning People, send your arrows to the middle of the earth. Hear the echo! Who is it? The People of the Spruce of the North. All your people and your thoughts come to us. Who is it? People of the white floating Clouds. Your thoughts come to us. All your people and your thoughts come to us. Who is it? The Lightning People. Your thoughts come to us. Who is it? Cloud People at the horizon. All your people and your thoughts come to us.

RAIN SONG

WHITE floating clouds. Clouds, like the plains, come and water the earth. Sun, embrace the earth that she may be fruitful. Moon, lion of the north, bear of the west, badger of the south, wolf of the east, eagle of the heavens, shrew of the earth, elder war hero, younger war hero, warriors of the six mountains of the world, intercede with the Cloud People for us that they may water the earth. Medicine bowl, cloud bowl, and water vase give us your hearts, that the earth may be watered. I make the ancient road of meal that my song may pass straight over it—the ancient road. White shell bead woman who lives where the sun goes down, mother whirlwind, father Sussistinnako, mother Yaya, creator of good thoughts, yellow woman of the north, blue woman of the west, red woman of the south, white woman of the east, slightly yellow woman of the zenith, and dark woman of the nadir, I ask your intercession with the Cloud People.

RAIN SONG

Sia (New Mexico)

LET the white floating clouds — the clouds like the plains — the lightning, thunder, rainbow, and cloud peoples, water the earth. Let the people of the white floating clouds,— the people of the clouds like the plains — the lightning, thunder, rainbow, and cloud peoples — come and work for us, and water the earth.

THE CORN MAIDENS

Zuni (New Mexico)

AFTER long ages of wandering, the precious Seed-things rested over the Middle at Zuni, and men turned their hearts to the cherishing of their corn and the Corn Maidens instead of warring with strange men.

But there was complaint by the people of the customs followed. Some said the music was not that of the olden time. Far better was that which of nights they often heard as they wandered up and down the river trail.[1] Wonderful music, as of liquid voices in caverns, or the echo of women's laughter in water-vases. And the music was timed with a deep-toned drum from the Mountain of Thunder. Others thought the music was that of the ghosts of ancient men, but it was far more beautiful than the music when danced the Corn Maidens. Others said light clouds rolled upward from the grotto in Thunder Mountain like to the mists that leave behind them the dew, but lo! even as they faded

[1] The mists and the dawn breeze on the river and in the grotto.

Zuni Ancestral Rock Gods

the bright garments of the Rainbow women might be seen fluttering, and the broidery and paintings of these dancers of the mist were more beautiful than the costumes of the Corn Maidens.

Then the priests of the people said, " It may well be Paiyatuma, the liquid voices his flute and the flutes of his players."

Now when the time of ripening corn was near, the fathers ordered preparation for the dance of the Corn Maidens. They sent the two Master-Priests of the Bow to the grotto at Thunder Mountains, saying, " If you behold Paiyatuma, and his maidens, perhaps they will give us the help of their customs."

Then up the river trail, the priests heard the sound of a drum and strains of song. It was Paiyatuma and his seven maidens, the Maidens of the House of Stars, sisters of the Corn Maidens.

The God of Dawn and Music lifted his flute and took his place in the line of dancers. The drum sounded until the cavern shook as with thunder. The flutes sang and sighed as the wind in a wooded cañon while still the storm is distant. White mists floated up from the wands of the Maidens, above which fluttered the butterflies of Summer-land about the dress of the Rainbows in the strange blue light of the night.

Then Paiyatuma, smiling, said, " Go the way before,

telling the fathers of our custom, and straightway we will follow."

Soon the sound of music was heard, coming from up the river, and soon the Flute People and singers and maidens of the Flute dance. Up rose the fathers and all the watching people, greeting the God of Dawn with outstretched hand and offering of prayer meal. Then the singers took their places and sounded their drum, flutes, and song of clear waters, while the Maidens of the Dew danced their Flute dance. Greatly marvelled the people, when from the wands they bore forth came white clouds, and fine cool mists descended.

Now when the dance was ended and the Dew Maidens had retired, out came the beautiful Mothers of Corn. And when the players of the flutes saw them, they were enamoured of their beauty and gazed upon them so intently that the Maidens let fall their hair and cast down their eyes. And jealous and bolder grew the mortal youths, and in the morning dawn, in rivalry, the dancers sought all too freely the presence of the Corn Maidens, no longer holding them so precious as in the olden time. And the matrons, intent on the new dance, heeded naught else. But behold! The mists increased greatly, surrounding dancers and watchers alike, until within them, the Maidens of Corn, all in white garments, became invisible. Then sadly and noiselessly they stole in amongst the people and laid their corn wands down amongst the trays, and laid their white broidered garments thereupon, as mothers lay soft kilting over their babes. Then even as the mists became they, and with the mists drifting, fled away, to the far south Summer-land.

THE SEARCH FOR THE CORN MAIDENS

Zuni (New Mexico)

THEN the people in their trouble called the two Master-Priests and said:

"Who, now, think ye, should journey to seek our precious Maidens? Bethink ye! Who amongst the Beings is even as ye are, strong of will and good of eyes? There is our great elder brother and father, Eagle, he of the floating down and of the terraced tail-fan. Surely he is enduring of will and surpassing of sight."

"Yea. Most surely," said the fathers. "Go ye forth and beseech him."

Then the two sped north to Twin Mountain, where in a grotto high up among the crags, with his mate and his young, dwelt the Eagle of the White Bonnet.

They climbed the mountain, but behold! Only the eaglets were there. They screamed lustily and tried to hide themselves in the dark recesses. "Pull not our feathers, ye of hurtful touch, but wait. When we are older we will drop them for you even from the clouds."

"Hush," said the warriors. "Wait in peace. We seek not ye but thy father."

Then from afar, with a frown, came old Eagle. "Why disturb ye my featherlings?" he cried.

"Behold! Father and elder brother, we come seeking only the light of thy favor. Listen!"

Then they told him of the lost Maidens of the Corn, and begged him to search for them.

"Be it well with thy wishes," said Eagle. "Go ye before contentedly."

So the warriors returned to the council. But Eagle winged his way high into the sky. High, high, he rose, until he circled among the clouds, small-seeming and swift, like seed-down in a whirlwind. Through all the heights, to the north, to the west, to the south, and to the east, he circled and sailed. Yet nowhere saw he trace of the Corn Maidens. Then he flew lower, returning. Before the warriors were rested, people heard the roar of his wings. As he alighted, the fathers said, "Enter thou and sit, oh brother, and say to us what thou hast to say." And they offered him the cigarette of the space relations.

When they had puffed the smoke toward the four points of the compass, and Eagle had purified his breath with smoke, and had blown smoke over sacred things, he spoke.

"Far have I journeyed, scanning all the regions. Neither bluebird nor woodrat can hide from my seeing," he said, snapping his beak. "Neither of them, unless they hide under bushes. Yet I have failed to see anything of the Maidens ye seek for. Send for my younger brother, the Falcon. Strong of flight is he, yet not so strong as I, and nearer the ground he takes his way ere sunrise."

Then the Eagle spread his wings and flew away to Twin Mountain. The Warrior-Priests of the Bow sped again fleetly over the plain to the westward for his younger brother, Falcon.

Sitting on an ant hill, so the warriors found Falcon. He paused as they approached, crying, "If ye have snare strings, I will be off like the flight of an arrow well plumed of our feathers!"

"No," said the priests. "Thy elder brother hath bidden us seek thee."

Then they told Falcon what had happened, and how Eagle had failed to find the Corn Maidens, so white and beautiful.

"Failed!" said Falcon. "Of course he failed. He climbs aloft to the clouds and thinks he can see under every bush and into every shadow, as sees the Sun-father who sees not with eyes. Go ye before."

Before the Warrior-Priests had turned toward the

town, the Falcon had spread his sharp wings and was skimming off over the tops of the trees and bushes as though verily seeking for field mice or birds' nests. And the Warriors returned to tell the fathers and to await his coming.

But after Falcon had searched over the world, to the north and west, to the east and south, he too returned and was received as had been Eagle. He settled on the edge of a tray before the altar, as on the ant hill he settles to-day. When he had smoked and had been smoked, as had been Eagle, he told the sorrowing fathers and mothers that he had looked behind every copse and cliff shadow, but of the Maidens he had found no trace.

"They are hidden more closely than ever sparrow hid," he said. Then he, too, flew away to his hills in the west.

"Our beautiful Maiden Mothers," cried the matrons. "Lost, lost as the dead are they!"

"Yes," said the others. "Where now shall we seek them? The far-seeing Eagle and the close-searching Falcon alike have failed to find them."

"Stay now your feet with patience," said the fathers. Some of them had heard Raven, who sought food in the refuse and dirt at the edge of town, at daybreak.

"Look now," they said. "There is Heavy-nose,

whose beak never fails to find the substance of seed itself, however little or well hidden it be. He surely must know of the Corn Maidens. Let us call him."

So the warriors went to the river side. When they found Raven, they raised their hands, all weaponless.

" We carry no pricking quills," they called. " Black-banded father, we seek your aid. Look now! The Mother-maidens of Seed whose substance is the food alike of thy people and our people, have fled away. Neither our grandfather the Eagle, nor his younger brother the Falcon, can trace them. We beg you to aid us or counsel us."

" Ka! ka! " cried the Raven. " Too hungry am I to go abroad fasting on business for ye. Ye are stingy! Here have I been since perching time, trying to find a throatful, but ye pick thy bones and lick thy bowls too clean for that, be sure."

" Come in, then, poor grandfather. We will give thee food to eat. Yea, and a cigarette to smoke, with all the ceremony."

" Say ye so? " said the Raven. He ruffled his collar and opened his mouth so wide with a lusty *kaw-la-ka-* that he might well have swallowed his own head. " Go ye before," he said, and followed them into the court of the dancers.

He was not ill to look upon. Upon his shoulders

THE LITTLE BASKET-MAKER

were bands of white cotton, and his back was blue, gleaming like the hair of a maiden dancer in the sunlight. The Master-Priest greeted Raven, bidding him sit and smoke.

"Ha! There is corn in this, else why the stalk of it?" said the Raven, when he took the cane cigarette of the far spaces and noticed the joint of it. Then he did as he had seen the Master-Priest do, only more greedily. He sucked in such a throatful of the smoke, fire and all, that it almost strangled him. He coughed and grew giddy, and the smoke all hot and stinging went through every part of him. It filled all his feathers, making even his brown eyes bluer and blacker, in rings. It is not to be wondered at, the blueness of flesh, blackness of dress, and skinniness, yes, and tearfulness of eye which we see in the Raven to-day. And they are all as greedy of corn food as ever, for behold! No sooner had the old Raven recovered than he espied one of the ears of corn half hidden under the mantle-covers of the trays. He leaped from his place laughing. They always laugh when they find anything, these ravens. Then he caught up the ear of corn and made off with it over the heads of the people and the tops of the houses, crying,

"Ha! ha! In this wise and in no other will ye find thy Seed Maidens."

But after a while he came back, saying, "A sharp eye have I for the flesh of the Maidens. But who might see their breathing-beings, ye dolts, except by the help of the Father of Dawn-Mist himself, whose breath makes breath of others seem as itself." Then he flew away cawing.

Then the elders said to each other, "It is our fault, so how dare we prevail on our father Paiyatuma to aid us? He warned us of this in the old time."

Suddenly, for the sun was rising, they heard Paiyatuma in his daylight mood and transformation. Thoughtless and loud, uncouth in speech, he walked along the outskirts of the village. He joked fearlessly even of fearful things, for all his words and deeds were the reverse of his sacred being. He sat down on a heap of vile refuse, saying he would have a feast.

"My poor little children," he said. But he spoke to aged priests and white-haired matrons.

"Good-night to you all," he said, though it was in full dawning. So he perplexed them with his speeches.

"We beseech thy favor, oh father, and thy aid, in finding our beautiful Maidens." So the priests mourned.

"Oh, that is all, is it? But why find that which is not lost, or summon those who will not come?"

Then he reproached them for not preparing the

sacred plumes, and picked up the very plumes he had said were not there.

Then the wise Pekwinna, the Speaker of the Sun, took two plumes and the banded wing-tips of the turkey, and approaching Paiyatuma stroked him with the tips of the feathers and then laid the feathers upon his lips. . . .

Then Paiyatuma became aged and grand and straight, as is a tall tree shorn by lightning. He said to the father:

"Thou are wise of thought and good of heart. Therefore I will summon from Summer-land the beautiful Maidens that ye may look upon them once more and make offering of plumes in sacrifice for them, but they are lost as dwellers amongst ye."

Then he told them of the song lines and the sacred speeches and of the offering of the sacred plume wands, and then turned him about and sped away so fleetly that none saw him.

Beyond the first valley of the high plain to the southward Paiyatuma planted the four plume wands. First he planted the yellow, bending over it and watching it. When it ceased to flutter, the soft down on it leaned northward but moved not. Then he set the blue wand and watched it; then the white wand. The eagle down on them leaned to right and left and still northward, yet moved not. Then farther on he planted the red wand, and bending low, without breathing, watched it closely. The soft down plumes began to wave as though blown by the breath of some small creature. Backward and forward, northward and southward they swayed, as if in time to the breath of one resting.

"'T is the breath of my Maidens in Summer-land, for the plumes of the southland sway soft to their gentle breathing. So shall it ever be. When I set the down of my mists on the plains and scatter my bright beads in the northland,[1] summer shall go thither from afar, borne on the breath of the Seed Maidens. Where they breathe, warmth, showers, and fertility shall follow with the birds of Summer-land, and the butterflies, northward over the world."

Then Paiyatuma arose and sped by the magic of his knowledge into the countries of Summer-land,—fled swiftly and silently as the soft breath he sought for, bearing his painted flute before him. And when he paused to rest, he played on his painted flute and the butterflies and birds sought him. So he sent them to seek the Maidens, following swiftly, and long before he found them he greeted them with the music of his song-sound, even as the People of the Seed now greet them in the song of the dancers.

[1] Dew drops.

When the Maidens heard his music and saw his tall form in their great fields of corn, they plucked ears, each of her own kind, and with them filled their colored trays and over all spread embroidered mantles, — embroidered in all the bright colors and with the creature-songs of Summer-land. So they sallied forth to meet him and welcome him. Then he greeted them, each with the touch of his hands and the breath of his flute, and bade them follow him to the northland home of their deserted children.

So by the magic of their knowledge they sped back as the stars speed over the world at night time, toward the home of our ancients. Only at night and dawn they journeyed, as the dead do, and the stars also. So they came at evening in the full of the last moon to the Place of the Middle, bearing their trays of seed.

Glorious was Paiyatuma, as he walked into the courts of the dancers in the dusk of the evening and stood with folded arms at the foot of the bow-fringed ladder of priestly council, he and his follower Shutsukya. He was tall and beautiful and banded with his own mists, and carried the banded wings of the turkeys with which he had winged his flight from afar, leading the Maidens, and followed as by his own shadow by the black being of the corn-soot, Shutsukya, who cries with the voice of the frost wind when the corn has grown aged and the harvest is taken away.

And surpassingly beautiful were the Maidens clothed in the white cotton and embroidered garments of Summer-land.

Then after long praying and chanting by the priests, the fathers of the people, and those of the Seed and Water, and the keepers of sacred things, the Maiden-mother of the North advanced to the foot of the ladder. She lifted from her head the beautiful tray of yellow corn and Paiyatama took it. He pointed it to the regions, each in turn, and the Priest of the North came and received the tray of sacred seed.

Then the Maiden of the West advanced and gave up her tray of blue corn. So each in turn the Maidens gave up their trays of precious seed. The Maiden of the South, the red seed; the Maiden of the East, the white seed; then the Maiden with the black seed, and lastly, the tray of all-color seed which the Priestess of Seed-and-All herself received.

And now, behold! The Maidens stood as before, she of the North at the northern end, but with her face southward far looking; she of the West, next, and lo! so all of them, with the seventh and last, looking southward. And standing thus, the darkness of the night fell around them. As shadows in deep night, so these Maidens of the Seed of Corn, the beloved and beautiful, were seen no more of men. And Paiyatuma stood alone, for Shutsukya walked now behind the Maidens, whistling shrilly, as the frost wind whistles when the corn is gathered away, among the lone canes and dry leaves of a gleaned field.

HASJELTI AND HOSTJOGHON

Navajo (New Mexico)

HASJELTI was the son of the white corn, and Hostjoghon the son of the yellow corn. They were born on the mountains where the fogs meet. These two became the great song-makers of the world.

To the mountain where they were born (Henry Mountain, Utah), they gave two songs and two prayers. Then they went to Sierra Blanca (Colorado) and made two songs and prayers and dressed the mountain in clothing of white shell with two eagle plumes upon its head. They visited San Mateo Mountain (New Mexico) and gave to it two songs and prayers, and dressed it in turquoise, even to leggings and moccasins, and placed two eagle plumes upon its head. Then they went to San Francisco Mountain (Arizona) and made two songs and prayers and dressed that mountain in abalone shells with two eagle plumes upon its head. They then visited Ute Mountain and gave to it two songs and prayers and dressed it in black beads. Then they returned to their own mountain where the fogs meet and said, "We two have made all these songs."

Courtesy of F. Ellerman, Mount Wilson Solar Observatory

"THEY WERE BORN ON THE MOUNTAINS WHERE THE FOGS MEET"

Apache Ollas

Other brothers were born of the white corn and yellow corn, and two brothers were placed on each mountain. They are the spirits of the mountains and to them the clouds come first. All the brothers together made game, the deer and elk and buffalo, and so game was created.

Navajos pray for rain and snow to Hasjelti and Hostjoghon. They stand upon the mountain tops and call the clouds to gather around them. Hasjelti prays to the sun, for the Navajos.

"Father, give me the light of your mind that my mind may be strong. Give me your strength, that my arm may be strong. Give me your rays, that corn and other vegetation may grow."

The most important prayers are addressed to Hasjelti and the most valuable gifts made to him. He talks to the Navajos through the birds, and for this reason the choicest feathers and plumes are placed in the cigarettes and attached to the prayer sticks offered to him.

THE SONG-HUNTER

Navajo (New Mexico)

A MAN sat thinking. "Let me see. My songs are too short. I want more songs. Where shall I go to find them?"

Hasjelti appeared and perceiving his thoughts, said, "I know where you can get more songs."

"Well, I want to get more. So I will follow you."

They went to a certain point in a box cañon in the Big Colorado River and here they found four gods, the Hostjobokon, at work, hewing cottonwood logs.

Hasjelti said, "This will not do. Cottonwood becomes water-soaked. You must use pine instead of cottonwood."

The Hostjobokon began boring the pine with flint, but Hasjelti said, "That is slow work." He commanded a whirlwind to hollow the log. A cross, joining at the exact middle of each log, a solid one and the hollow one, was formed. The arms of the cross were equal.

The song-hunter entered the hollow log and Hasjelti closed the end with a cloud so that water would not enter when the logs were launched upon the great waters. The logs floated off. The Hostjobokon, accompanied by their wives, rode upon the logs, one couple sitting upon each arm. Hasjelti, Hostjoghon, and the two Naaskiddi walked upon the banks to keep the logs off shore. Hasjelti carried a squirrel skin filled with tobacco, with which to supply the gods on their journey. Hostjoghon carried a staff ornamented with eagle and turkey plumes and a gaming ring with two humming birds tied to it with white cotton cord. The two Naaskiddi carried staffs of lightning. The Naaskiddi had clouds upon their backs in which the seeds of all corn and grasses were carried.

After floating a long distance down the river, they came to waters that had a shore on one side only. Here they landed. Here they found a people like themselves. When these people learned of the Song-hunter, they gave him many songs and they painted pictures on a cotton blanket and said,

"These pictures must go with the songs. If we give this blanket to you, you will lose it. We will give you white earth and black coals which you will grind together to make black paint, and we will give you white sand, yellow sand, and red sand. For the blue paint you will take white sand and black coals with a very little red and yellow sand. These will give you blue."

And so the Navajo people make blue, even to this day.

The Song-hunter remained with these people until the corn was ripe. There he learned to eat corn and he carried some back with him to the Navajos, who had not seen corn before, and he taught them how to raise it and how to eat it.

When he wished to return home, the logs would not float upstream. Four sunbeams attached themselves to the logs, one to each cross arm, and so drew the Song-hunter back to the box cañon from which he had started. When he reached that point, he separated the logs. He placed the end of the solid log into the hollow end of the other and planted this great pole in the river. It may be seen there to-day by the venturesome. In early days many went there to pray and make offerings.

SAND PAINTING OF THE SONG-HUNTER

Navajo

(Explanatory of frontispiece)

THE black cross bars denote pine logs; the white lines the froth of the water; the yellow, vegetable debris gathered by the logs; the blue and red lines, sunbeams. The blue spot in the centre of the cross denotes water. There are four Hostjo-bokon, with their wives, the Hostjoboard. Each couple sits upon one of the cross arms of the logs. The gods carry in their right hands a rattle, and in their left sprigs of piñon; the goddesses carry piñon sprigs in both hands.

Hasjelti is to the east of the painting. He carries a squirrel skin filled with tobacco. His shirt is white cotton and very elastic. The leggings are of white deer-skin, fringed, and his head is ornamented with an eagle's tail; at the tip of each plume there is a fluffy feather from the breast of the eagle. The projection on the right of the throat is a fox skin.

Hostjoghon is at the west. His shirt is invisible, the dark being the dark of the body. His staff is colored black from a charred plant. Two strips of beaver skin tipped with six quills of the porcupine are attached to the right of the throat. The four colored stars on the body are bead ornaments. The top of the staff is ornamented with a turkey's tail. Eagle and turkey plumes are alternately attached to the staff.

The Naaskiddi are north and south of the painting. They carry staffs of lightning ornamented with eagle plumes and sunbeams. Their bodies are nude except the loin skirt. The hunch upon the back is a black cloud and the three groups of white lines indicate corn and other seeds. Five eagle plumes are attached to the cloud-back, since eagles live among the clouds. The body is surrounded by sunlight. The lines of blue and red which border the cloud-back denote sunbeams penetrating storm clouds. The black circle zig-zagged with white around the head is a cloud basket filled with corn and seeds of grass. On each side of the head are five feathers of the red-shafted flicker.

The Rainbow goddess, upon which these gods often travel, partly encircles and completes the picture.

These sand pictures are drawn upon common yellow sand, brought in blankets and laid in squares about three inches thick and four feet in diameter. The colors used in decoration were yellow, red, and white, secured from sand stones, black from charcoal, and a grayish blue made from white sand and charcoal mixed with a very small quantity of yellow and red sands.

(From eighth annual report of the Bureau of Ethnology, abridged from description of James Stevenson.)

THE GUIDING DUCK AND THE LAKE OF DEATH

Zuni (New Mexico)

NOW K-yak-lu, the all-hearing and wise of speech, all alone had been journeying afar in the North Land of cold and white loneliness. He was lost, for the world in which he wandered was buried in the snow which lies spread there forever. So cold he was that his face became wan and white from the frozen mists of his own breath, white as become all creatures who dwell there. So cold at night and dreary of heart, so lost by day and blinded by the light was he that he wept, and died of heart and became transformed as are the gods. Yet his lips called continually and his voice grew shrill and dry-sounding, like the voice of far-flying water-fowl. As he cried, wandering blindly, the water birds flocking around him peered curiously at him, calling meanwhile to their comrades. But wise though he was of all speeches, and their meanings plain to him, yet none told him the way to his country and people.

Now the Duck heard his cry and it was like her own.

Courtesy of F. Ellerman, Mount Wilson Solar Observatory

". . . IN THE NORTHLAND OF COLD AND WHITE LONELINESS"

She was of all regions the traveller and searcher, knowing all the ways, whether above or below the waters, whether in the north, the west, the south, or the east, and was the most knowing of all creatures. Thus the wisdom of the one understood the knowledge of the other.

And the All-wise cried to her, "The mountains are white and the valleys; all plains are like others in whiteness, and even the light of our Father the Sun, makes all ways more hidden of whiteness! In brightness my eyes see but darkness."

The Duck answered:

"Think no longer sad thoughts. Thou hearest all as I see all. Give me tinkling shells from thy girdle and place them on my neck and in my beak. I may guide thee with my seeing if thou hear and follow my trail. Well I know the way to thy country. Each year I lead thither the wild geese and the cranes who flee there as winter follows."

So the All-wise placed his talking shells on the neck of the Duck, and the singing shells in her beak, and though painfully and lamely, yet he followed the sound she made with the shells. From place to place with swift flight she sped, then awaiting him, ducking her head that the shells might call loudly. By and by they came to the country of thick rains and mists on the borders of the Snow World, and passed from water to water, until wider water lay in their path. In vain the Duck called and jingled the shells from the midst of the waters. K-yak-lu could neither swim nor fly as could the Duck.

Now the Rainbow-worm was near in that land of mists and waters and he heard the sound of the sacred shells.

"These be my grandchildren," he said, and called, "Why mourn ye? Give me plumes of the spaces. I will bear you on my shoulders."

Then the All-wise took two of the lightest plume-wands, and the Duck her two strong feathers. And he fastened them together and breathed on them while the Rainbow-worm drew near. The Rainbow unbent himself that K-yak-lu might mount, then he arched himself high among the clouds. Like an arrow he straightened himself forward, and followed until his face looked into the Lake of the Ancients. And there the All-wise descended, and sat there alone, in the plain beyond the mountains. The Duck had spread her wings in flight to the south to take counsel of the gods.

Then the Duck, even as the gods had directed, prepared a litter of poles and reeds, and before the morning came, with the litter they went, singing a quaint and pleasant song, down the northern plain. And when they found the All-wise, he looked upon them in the starlight and wept. But the father of the gods stood over him and chanted the sad dirge rite. Then K-yak-lu sat down in the great soft litter they bore for him.

They lifted it upon their shoulders, bearing it lightly, singing loudly as they went, to the shores of the deep black lake, where gleamed from the middle the lights of the dead.

Out over the magic ladder of rushes and canes which reared itself over the water, they bore him. And K-yak-lu, scattering sacred prayer meal before him, stepped down the way, slowly, like a blind man. No sooner had he taken four steps than the ladder lowered into the deep. And the All-wise entered the council room of the gods.

The gods sent out their runners, to summon all beings, and called in dancers for the Dance of Good. And with these came the little ones who had sunk beneath the waters, well and beautiful and all seemingly clad in cotton mantles and precious neck jewels.

THE BOY WHO BECAME A GOD

Navajo (New Mexico)

THE Tolchini, a clan of the Navajos, lived at Wind Mountains. One of them used to take long visits into the country. His brothers thought he was crazy. The first time on his return, he brought with him a pine bough; the second time, corn. Each time he returned he brought something new and had a strange story to tell. His brothers said: "He is crazy. He does not know what he is talking about."

Now the Tolchini left Wind Mountains and went to a rocky foothill east of the San Mateo Mountain. They had nothing to eat but seed grass. The eldest brother said, "Let us go hunting," but they told the youngest brother not to leave camp. But five days and five nights passed, and there was no word. So he followed them.

After a day's travel he camped near a cañon, in a cavelike place. There was much snow but no water so he made a fire and heated a rock, and made a hole in the ground. The hot rock heated the snow and gave him water to drink. Just then he heard a tumult over his head, like people passing. He went out to see what made the noise and saw many crows crossing back and forth over the cañon. This was the home of the crow, but there were other feathered people there, and the chaparral cock. He saw many fires made by the crows on each side of the cañon. Two crows flew down near him and the youth listened to hear what was the matter.

The two crows cried out, "Somebody says. Somebody says."

The youth did not know what to make of this.

A crow on the opposite side called out, "What is the matter? Tell us! Tell us! What is wrong?"

The first two cried out, "Two of us got killed. We met two of our men who told us."

Then they told the crows how two men who were out hunting killed twelve deer, and a party of the Crow People went to the deer after they were shot. They said, "Two of us who went after the blood of the deer were shot."

The crows on the other side of the cañon called, "Which men got killed?"

"The chaparral cock, who sat on the horn of the deer, and the crow who sat on its backbone."

The others called out, "We are not surprised they

were killed. That is what we tell you all the time. If you go after dead deer you must expect to be killed."

"We will not think of them longer," so the two crows replied. "They are dead and gone. We are talking of things of long ago."

But the youth sat quietly below and listened to everything that was said.

After a while the crows on the other side of the cañon made a great noise and began to dance. They had many songs at that time. The youth listened all the time. After the dance a great fire was made and he could see black objects moving, but he could not distinguish any people. He recognized the voice of Hasjelti. He remembered everything in his heart. He even remembered the words of the songs that continued all night. He remembered every word of every song. He said to himself, "I will listen until daylight."

The Crow People did not remain on the side of the cañon where the fires were first built. They crossed and recrossed the cañon in their dance. They danced back and forth until daylight. Then all the crows and the other birds flew away to the west. All that was left was the fires and the smoke.

Then the youth started for his brothers' camp. They saw him coming. They said, "He will have lots of stories to tell. He will say he saw something no one ever saw."

But the brother-in-law who was with them said, "Let him alone. When he comes into camp he will tell us all. I believe these things do happen for he could not make up these things all the time."

Now the camp was surrounded by piñon brush and a large fire was burning in the centre. There was much meat roasting over the fire. When the youth reached the camp, he raked over the coals and said. "I feel cold."

Brother-in-law replied, "It is cold. When people camp together, they tell stories to one another in the morning. We have told ours, now you tell yours."

The youth said, "Where I stopped last night was the worst camp I ever had." The brothers paid no attention but the brother-in-law listened.

The youth said, "I never heard such a noise." Then he told his story. Brother-in-law asked what kind of people made the noise.

The youth said, "I do not know. They were strange people to me, but they danced all night back and forth across the cañon and I heard them say my brothers killed twelve deer and afterwards killed two of their people who went for the blood of the deer. I heard them say, "'That is what must be expected. If you go to such places, you must expect to be killed.'"

The elder brother began thinking. He said, " How many deer did you say were killed? "

" Twelve."

Elder brother said, " I never believed you before, but this story I do believe. How do you find out all these things? What is the matter with you that you know them? "

The boy said, " I do not know. They come into my mind and to my eyes."

Then they started homeward, carrying the meat. The youth helped them.

As they were descending a mesa, they sat down on the edge to rest. Far down the mesa were four mountain sheep. The brothers told the youth to kill one.

The youth hid in the sage brush and when the sheep came directly toward him, he aimed his arrow at them. But his arm stiffened and became dead. The sheep passed by.

He headed them off again by hiding in the stalks of a large yucca. The sheep passed within five steps of him, but again his arm stiffened as he drew the bow.

He followed the sheep and got ahead of them and hid behind a birch tree in bloom. He had his bow ready, but as they neared him they became gods. The first was Hasjelti, the second was Hostjoghon, the third was Naaskiddi, and the fourth Hadatchishi. Then the youth fell senseless to the ground.

Courtesy of Smithsonian Institution

NAVAJO BLANKET WEAVING

The four gods stood one on each side of him, each with a rattle. They traced with their rattles in the sand the figure of a man, drawing lines at his head and feet. Then the youth recovered and the gods again became sheep. They said, "Why did you try to shoot us? You see you are one of us." For the youth had become a sheep.

The gods said, "There is to be a dance, far off to the north beyond the Ute Mountain. We want you to go with us. We will dress you like ourselves and teach you to dance. Then we will wander over the world."

Now the brothers watched from the top of the mesa but they could not see what the trouble was. They saw the youth lying on the ground, but when they reached the place, all the sheep were gone. They began crying, saying, "For a long time we would not believe him, and now he has gone off with the sheep."

They tried to head off the sheep, but failed. They said, "If we had believed him, he would not have gone off with the sheep. But perhaps some day we will see him again."

At the dance, the five sheep found seven others. This made their number twelve. They journeyed all around the world. All people let them see their dances and learn their songs. Then the eleven talked together and said,

"There is no use keeping this youth with us longer. He has learned everything. He may as well go back to his people and teach them to do as we do."

So the youth was taught to have twelve in the dance, six gods and six goddesses, with Hasjelti to lead them. He was told to have his people make masks to represent the gods.

So the youth returned to his brothers, carrying with him all songs, all medicines, and clothing.

ORIGIN OF CLEAR LAKE

Patwin (Sacramento Valley, Cal.)

BEFORE anything was created at all, Old Frog and Old Badger lived alone together. Old Badger wanted to drink, so Old Frog gnawed into a tree, drew out all the sap and put it in a hollow place. Then he created Little Frogs to help him, and working together they dug out the lake.

Then Old Frog made the little flat whitefish. Some of them lived in the lake, but others swam down Cache Creek, and turned into the salmon, pike, and sturgeon which swim in the Sacramento.

THE GREAT FIRE

Patwin (Sacramento Valley, Cal.)

LONG ago a man loved two women and wished to marry both of them. But the women were magpies and they laughed at him. Therefore the man went to the north, and made for himself a tule boat. Then he set the world on fire, and himself escaped to sea in his boat.

But the fire burned with terrible speed. It ate its way into the south. It licked up all things on earth, men, trees, rocks, animals, water, and even the ground itself.

Now Old Coyote saw the burning and the smoke from his place far in the south, and he ran with all his might to put it out. He put two little boys in a sack and ran north like the wind. He took honey-dew into his mouth, chewed it up, spat on the fire, and so put it out. Now the fire was out, but there was no water and Coyote was thirsty. So he took Indian sugar again, chewed it up, dug a hole in the bottom of the creek, covered up the sugar in it, and it turned to water and filled the creek. So the earth had water again.

But the two little boys cried because they were lonesome, for there was nobody left on earth. Then Coyote made a sweat house, and split a number of sticks, and laid them in the sweat house over night. In the morning they had all turned into men and women.

ORIGIN OF THE RAVEN AND THE MACAW
(Totems of summer and winter)

Zuni (New Mexico)

THE priest who was named Yanauluha carried ever in his hand a staff which now in the daylight was plumed and covered with feathers — yellow, blue-green, red, white, black, and varied. Attached to it were shells, which made a song-like tinkle. The people when they saw it stretched out their hands and asked many questions.

Then the priest balanced it in his hand, and struck with it a hard place, and blew upon it. Amid the plumes appeared four round things — mere eggs they were. Two were blue like the sky and two dun-red like the flesh of the Earth-mother.

Then the people asked many questions.

"These," said the priests, "are the seed of living beings. Choose which ye will follow. From two eggs shall come beings of beautiful plumage, colored like the grass and fruits of summer. Where they fly and ye follow, shall always be summer. Without toil, fields of food shall flourish. And from the other two eggs shall come evil beings, piebald, with white, without

Zuni Pueblo from the Southeast

Climbing up the Acoma Trail

colors. And where these two shall fly and ye shall follow, winter strives with summer. Only by labor shall the fields yield fruit, and your children and theirs shall strive for the fruits. Which do ye choose?"

"The blue! The blue!" cried the people, and those who were strongest carried off the blue eggs, leaving the red eggs to those who waited. They laid the blue eggs with much gentleness in soft sand on the sunny side of a hill, watching day by day. They were precious of color; surely they would be the precious birds of the Summer-land. Then the eggs cracked and the birds came out, with open eyes and pin feathers under their skins.

"We chose wisely," said the people. "Yellow and blue, red and green, are their dresses, even seen through their skins." So they fed them freely of all the foods which men favor. Thus they taught them to eat all desirable food. But when the feathers appeared, they were black with white bandings. They were ravens. And they flew away croaking hoarse laughs and mocking our fathers.

But the other eggs became beautiful macaws, and were wafted by a toss of the priest's wand to the far-away Summer-land.

So those who had chosen the raven, became the Raven People. They were the Winter People and they were many and strong. But those who had chosen the macaw, became the Macaw People. They were the Summer People, and few in number, and less strong, but they were wiser because they were more deliberate. The priest Yanauluha, being wise, became their father, even as the Sun-father is among the little moons of the sky. He and his sisters were the ancestors of the priest-keepers of things.

COYOTE AND THE HARE

Sia (New Mexico)

ONE day Coyote was passing about when he saw Hare sitting before his house. Coyote thought, "In a minute I will catch you," and he sprang and caught Hare.

Hare cried, "Man Coyote, do not eat me. Wait just a minute; I have something to tell you — something you will be glad to hear — something you must hear."

"Well," said Coyote, "I will wait."

"Let me sit at the entrance of my house," said Hare. "Then I can talk to you."

Coyote allowed Hare to take his seat at the entrance.

Hare said, "What are you thinking of, Coyote?"

"Nothing," said Coyote.

"Listen, then," said Hare. "I am a hare and I am very much afraid of people. When they come carrying arrows, I am afraid of them. When they see me they aim their arrows at me and I am afraid, and oh! how I tremble!"

Hare began trembling violently until he saw Coyote

a little off his guard, then he began to run. It took Coyote a minute to think and then he ran after Hare, but always a little behind. Hare raced away and soon entered a house, just in time to escape Coyote. Coyote tried to enter the house but found it was hard stone. He became very angry.

Coyote cried, "I was very stupid! Why did I allow this Hare to fool me? I must have him. But this house is so strong, how can I open it?"

Coyote began to work, but after a while he said to himself, "The stone is so strong I cannot open it."

Presently Hare called, "Man Coyote, how are you going to kill me?"

"I know how," said Coyote. "I will kill you with fire."

"Where is the wood?" asked Hare, for he knew there was no wood at his house.

"I will bring grass," said Coyote, "and set fire to it. The fire will enter your house and kill you."

"Oh," said Hare, "but the grass is mine. It is my food; it will not kill me. It is my friend. The grass will not kill me."

"Then," said Coyote, "I will bring all the trees of the wood and set fire to them."

"All the trees know me," said Hare. "They are my friends. They will not kill me. They are my food."

Photo by Charles Albertson

PIÑON TREE IN THE GRAND CAÑON

Putnam & Valentine

SAN XAVIER MISSION, TUCSON, ARIZONA

Coyote thought a minute. Then he said, "I will bring the gum of the piñon and set fire to that."

Hare said, "Now I am afraid. I do not eat that. It is not my friend."

Coyote rejoiced that he had thought of a plan for getting the hare. He hurried and brought all the gum he could carry and placed it at the door of Hare's house and set fire to it. In a short time the gum boiled like hot grease, and Hare cried,

"Now I know I shall die! What shall I do?" Yet all the time he knew what he would do.

But Coyote was glad Hare was afraid. After a while Hare called, "The fire is entering my house," and Coyote answered, "Blow it out!"

But Coyote drew nearer and blew with all his might to blow the flame into Hare's house

Hare cried, "You are so close you are blowing the fire on me and I will soon be burned."

Coyote was so happy that he drew closer and blew harder, and drew still closer so that his face was very close to Hare's face. Then Hare suddenly threw the boiling gum into Coyote's face and escaped from his house.

It took Coyote a long time to remove the gum from his face, and he felt very sorrowful. He said, "I am very, very stupid."

COYOTE AND THE QUAILS

Pima (*Arizona*)

ONCE upon a time, long ago, Coyote was sleeping so soundly that a covey of quails came along and cut pieces of fat meat out of his flesh without arousing him. Then they went on. After they had camped for the evening, and were cooking the meat, Coyote came up the trail.

Coyote said, "Where did you get that nice, fat meat? Give me some."

Quails gave him all he wanted. Then he went farther up the trail. After he had gone a little way, Quails called to him,

"Coyote, you were eating your own flesh."

Coyote said, "What did you say?"

Quails said, "Oh, nothing. We heard something calling behind the mountains."

Soon the quails called again: "Coyote, you ate your own meat."

"What did you say?"

"Oh, nothing. We heard somebody pounding his grinding-stone."

So Coyote went on. But at last he began to feel where he had been cut. Then he knew what the quails meant. He turned back down the trail and told Quails he would eat them up. He began to chase them. The quails flew above ground and Coyote ran about under them. At last they got tired, but Coyote did not because he was so angry.

By and by Quails came to a hole, and one of the keenest-witted picked up a piece of prickly cholla cactus and pushed it into the hole; then they all ran in after it. But Coyote dug out the hole and reached them. When he came to the first quail he said,

"Was it you who told me I ate my own flesh?"

Quail said, "No."

So Coyote let him go and he flew away. When Coyote came to the second quail, he asked the same question. Quail said, "No," and then flew away. So Coyote asked every quail, until the last quail was gone, and then he came to the cactus branch. Now the prickly cactus branch was so covered with feathers that it looked just like a quail. Coyote asked it the same question, but the cactus branch did not answer. Then Coyote said,

"I know it was you because you do not answer."

So Coyote bit very hard into the hard, prickly branch, and it killed him.

COYOTE AND THE FAWNS

Sia (New Mexico)

ANOTHER day when he was travelling around, Coyote met a deer with two fawns. The fawns were beautifully spotted, and he said to the deer, "How did you paint your children? They are so beautiful!"

Deer replied, "I painted them with fire from the cedar."

"And how did you do the work?" asked Coyote.

"I put my children into a cave and built a fire of cedar in front of it. Every time a spark flew from the fire it struck my children, making a beautiful spot."

"Oh," said Coyote, "I will do the same thing. Then I will make my children beautiful."

He hurried to his house and put his children in a cave. Then he built a fire of cedar in front of it and stood off to watch the fire. But the children cried because the fire was very hot. Coyote kept calling to them not to cry because they would be beautiful like the deer. After a time the crying ceased and Coyote was pleased. But when the fire died down, he found they were burned to death. Coyote expected to find them beautiful, but instead they were dead.

Then he was enraged with the deer and ran away to hunt her, but he could not find her anywhere. He was much distressed to think the deer had fooled him so easily.

HOW THE BLUEBIRD GOT ITS COLOR

Pima (Arizona)

A LONG time ago, the bluebird was a very ugly color. But Bluebird knew of a lake where no river flowed in or out, and he bathed in this four times every morning for four mornings. Every morning he sang a magic song:

> "There 's a blue water. It lies there.
> I went in.
> I am all blue."

On the fourth morning Bluebird shed all his feathers and came out of the lake just in his skin. But the next morning when he came out of the lake he was covered with blue feathers.

Now all this while Coyote had been watching Bluebird. He wanted to jump in and get him to eat, but he was afraid of the water. But on that last morning Coyote said,

"How is it you have lost all your ugly color, and now you are blue and gay and beautiful? You are more beautiful than anything that flies in the air. I want to be blue, too." Now Coyote at that time was a bright green.

Department of Botanical Research, Carnegie Institution of Washington

MESQUITE AND SMALL CEREUS CACTUS

Courtesy of Smithsonian Institution

VASES WITH FIGURES OF BUTTERFLIES, FROM SIKYATKI

"I only went in four times on four mornings," said Bluebird. He taught Coyote the magic song, and he went in four times, and the fifth time he came out as blue as the little bird.

Then Coyote was very, very proud because he was a blue coyote. He was so proud that as he walked along he looked around on every side to see if anybody was looking at him now that he was a blue coyote and so beautiful. He looked to see if his shadow was blue, too. But Coyote was so busy watching to see if others were noticing him that he did not watch the trail. By and by he ran into a stump so hard that it threw him down in the dirt and he was covered with dust all over. You may know this is true because even to-day coyotes are the color of dirt.

COYOTE'S EYES

Pima (Arizona)

WHEN Coyote was travelling about one day, he saw a small bird. The bird was hopping about contentedly and Coyote thought,

"What a beautiful bird. It moves about so gracefully."

He drew nearer to the bird and asked, "What beautiful things are you working with?" but the bird could not understand Coyote. After a while the bird took out his two eyes and threw them straight up into the air, like two stones. It looked upward but had no eyes. Then the bird said,

"Come, my eyes. Come quickly, down into my head." The eyes fell down into the bird's head, just where they belonged, but were much brighter than before.

Coyote thought he could brighten his eyes. He asked the bird to take out his eyes. The bird took out Coyote's eyes, held them for a moment in his hands, and threw them straight up into the air. Coyote looked up and called,

"Come back, my eyes. Come quickly." They at once fell back into his head and were much brighter than before. Coyote wanted to try it again, but the bird did not wish to. But Coyote persisted. Then the bird said,

"Why should I work for you, Coyote? No, I will work no more for you." But Coyote still persisted, and the bird took out his eyes and threw them up. Coyote cried,

"Come, my eyes, come back to me."

But his eyes continued to rise into the air, and the bird began to go away. Coyote began to weep. But the bird was annoyed, and called back,

"Go away now. I am tired of you. Go away and get other eyes."

But Coyote refused to go and entreated the bird to find eyes for him. At last the bird gathered gum from a piñon tree and rolled it between his hands and put it in Coyote's eye holes, so that he could see. But his eyes had been black and very bright. His new eyes were yellow.

"Now," said the bird, "go away. You cannot stay here any longer."

COYOTE AND THE TORTILLAS

Pima (Arizona)

ONCE upon a time, a river rose very high and spread all over the land. An Indian woman was going along the trail by the river side with a basket of tortillas on her head, but she was wading in water up to her waist. Now Coyote was afraid of the water, so he had climbed into a cottonwood tree. When the woman came up the trail, Coyote called,

"Oh, come to this tree and give me some of those nice tortillas."

The woman said, "No. I can't give them to you; they are for somebody else."

"If you do not come here I will shoot you," said Coyote, and the woman really thought he had a bow. So she came to the tree and said, "You must come down and get them. I can't climb trees."

Coyote came down as far as he dared, but he was afraid of the deep water. The woman laughed at him. She said, "Just see how shallow it is. It's only up to my ankles." But she was standing on a big stump. Coyote looked at the water. It seemed shallow and safe enough, so he jumped. But the water was deep and he was drowned. Then the woman went on up the trail.

COYOTE AS A HUNTER

Sia (New Mexico)

COYOTE travelled a long distance and in the middle of the day it was very hot. He sat down and rested, and thought, as he looked up to Tinia, "How I wish the Cloud People would freshen my path and make it cool."

In just a little while the Cloud People gathered over the trail Coyote was following and he was glad that his path was to be cool and shady.

After he travelled some distance further, he sat down again and looking upward said, "I wish the Cloud People would send rain. My road would be cooler and fresher." In a little while a shower came and Coyote was contented.

But in a short time he again sat down and wished that the road could be very moist, that it would be fresh to his feet, and almost immediately the trail was as wet as though a river had passed over it. Again Coyote was contented.

But after a while he took his seat again. He said to himself, "I guess I will talk again to the Cloud People." Then he looked up and said to them,

" I wish for water over my road — water to my elbows, that I may travel on my hands and feet in the cool waters; then I shall be refreshed and happy."

In a short time his road was covered with water, and he moved on. But again he wished for something more, and said to the Cloud People,

" I wish much for water to my shoulders. Then I will be happy and contented."

In a moment the waters arose as he wished, yet after a while he looked up and said, " If you will only give me water so high that my eyes, nose, mouth and ears are above it, I will be happy. Then indeed my road will be cool."

But even this did not satisfy him, and after travelling a while longer he implored the Cloud People to give him a river that he might float over the trail, and immediately a river appeared and Coyote floated down stream. Now he had been high in the mountains and wished to go to Hare Land.

After floating a long distance, he at last came to Hare Land and saw many Hares a little distance off, on both sides of the river. Coyote lay down in the mud as though he were dead and listened. Soon a woman ka-wate (*mephitis*) came along with a vase and a gourd for water.

She said, " Here is a dead coyote. Where did he

come from? I guess from the mountains above. I guess he fell into the water and died."

Coyote looked up and said, "Come here, woman."

She said, "What do you want?"

Coyote said, "I know the Hares and other small animals well. In a little while they will come here and think I am dead and be happy. What do you think about it?"

Ka-wate said, "I have no thoughts at all."

So Coyote explained his plan. . . .

So Coyote lay as dead, and all the Hares and small animals saw him lying in the river, and rejoiced that he was dead. The Hares decided to go in a body and see the dead Coyote. Rejoicing over his death, they struck him with their hands and kicked him. There were crowds of Hares and they decided to have a great dance. Now and then a dancing Hare would stamp upon Coyote who lay as if dead. During the dance the Hares clapped their hands over their mouth and gave a whoop like a war-whoop.

Then Coyote rose quickly and took two clubs which the ka-wate had given him, and together they killed all of the Hares. There was a great number and they were piled up like stones.

Coyote said, "Where shall I find fire to cook the hares? Ah," he said, pointing across to a high rock,

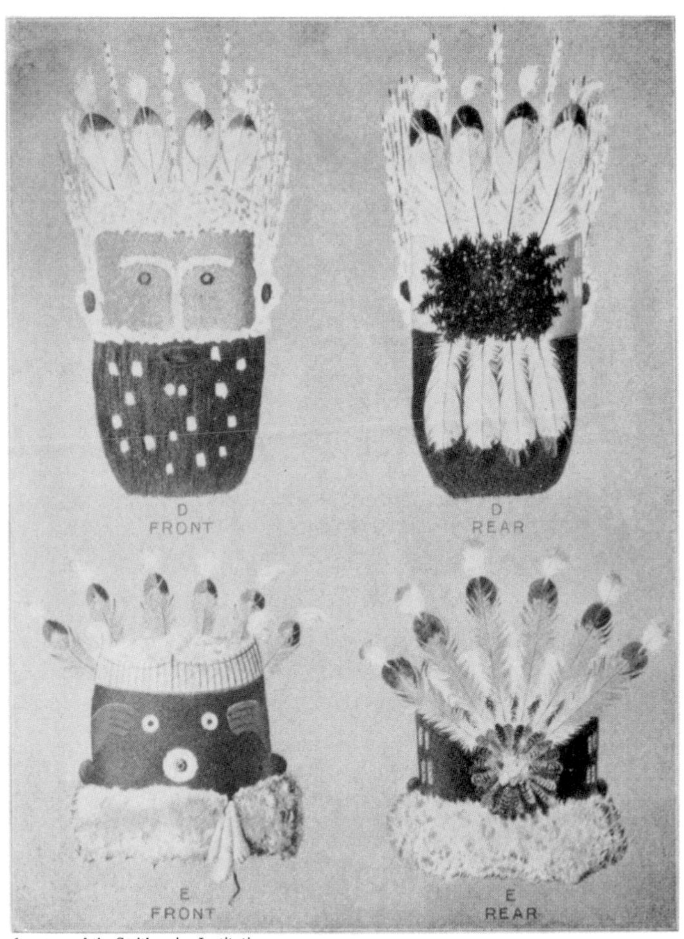

Courtesy of the Smithsonian Institution

SIA MASKS

"that rock gives good shade and it is cool. I will find fire and cook my meat in the shade of that rock."

So they carried all the hares to that point and Coyote made a large fire and threw them into it. When he had done this he was very warm and tired. He lay down close to the rock in the shade.

After a while he said to Ka-wate, "We will run a race. The one who wins will have all the hares."

She said, "How could I beat you? Your feet are so much larger than mine."

Coyote said, "I will allow you the start of me." He made a torch of the inner shreds of cedar bark and wrapped it with yucca thread and lighted it. Then he tied this torch to the end of his tail. He did this to see that the ka-wate did not escape him.

Ka-wate started first, but when out of sight of Coyots, she slipped into the house of Badger. Then Coyote started with the fire attached to his tail. Wherever he touched the grass, he set fire to it. But Ka-wate hurried back to the rock, carried all the hares on top except four tiny ones, and then climbed up on the rock.

Coyote was surprised not to overtake her. He said, "She must be very quick. How could she run so fast?" Then he returned to the rock, but did not see her.

He was tired and sat down in the shade of the rock.

"Why does n't she come?" he said. "Perhaps she will not come before night, her feet are so small."

Ka-wate sat on the rock above and heard all he said. She watched him take a stick and look into the mound for the hares. He pulled out a small one which he threw away. But the second was smaller than the first. Then a third and a fourth, each tiny, and all he threw away. "I do not care for the smaller ones," he said. "There are so many here, I will not eat the little ones." But he hunted and hunted in the mound of ashes for the hares. All were gone.

He said, "That woman has robbed me." Then he picked up the four little ones and ate them. He looked about for Ka-wate but did not see her because he did not look up. Then as he was tired and lay down to rest, he looked up and saw her, with the cooked hares piled beside her.

Coyote was hungry. He begged her to throw one down. She threw a very small one. Then Coyote became angry. And he was still more angry because he could not climb the rock. She had gone where he could not go.

HOW THE RATTLESNAKE LEARNED TO BITE

Pima (Arizona)

AFTER people and the animals were created, they all lived together. Rattlesnake was there, and was called Soft Child because he was so soft in his motions. The people liked to hear him rattle and little rest did he get because they continually poked and scratched him so that he would shake the rattles in his tail. At last Rattlesnake went to Elder Brother to ask help. Elder Brother pulled a hair from his own lip, cut it in short pieces, and made it into teeth for Soft Child.

" If any one bothers you," he said, " bite him."

That very evening Ta-api, Rabbit, came to Soft Child as he had done before and scratched him. Soft Child raised his head and bit Rabbit. Rabbit was angry and scratched again. Soft Child bit him again. Then Rabbit ran about saying that Soft Child was angry and had bitten him. Then he went to Rattlesnake again, and twice more he was bitten.

The bites made Rabbit very sick. He asked for a

bed of cool sea sand. Coyote was sent to the sea for the cool, damp sand. Then Rabbit asked for the shade of bushes that he might feel the cool breeze. But at last Rabbit died. He was the first creature which had died in this new world.

Then the people were troubled because they did not know what to do with the body of Rabbit. One said, "If we bury him, Coyote will surely dig him up."

Another said, "If we hide him, Coyote will surely find him."

And another said, "If we put him in a tree, Coyote will surely climb up."

So they decided to burn the body of Rabbit, and yet there was no fire on earth.

Blue Fly said, "Go to Sun and get some of the fire which he keeps in his house," So Coyote scampered away, but he was sure the people were trying to get rid of him so he kept looking back.

Then Blue Fly made the first fire drill. Taking a stick like an arrow he twirled it in his hands, letting the lower end rest on a flat stick that lay on the ground. Soon smoke began to arise, and then fire came. The people gathered fuel and began their duty.

But Coyote, looking back, saw fire ascending. He turned and ran back as fast as he could go. When the people saw him coming, they formed a ring, but he raced around the circle until he saw two short men standing together. He jumped over them, and seized the heart of Rabbit. But he burned his mouth doing it, and it is black to this day.

COYOTE AND THE RATTLESNAKE

Sia (New Mexico)

COYOTE'S house was not far from Rattlesnake's home. One morning when they were out walking together, Coyote said to Rattlesnake,

" To-morrow come to my house."

In the morning Rattlesnake went to Coyote's house. He moved slowly along the floor, shaking his rattle. Coyote sat at one side, very much frightened. The movements of the snake and the rattle frightened him. Coyote had a pot of rabbit meat on the fire, which he placed in front of the snake, saying,

" Companion, eat."

" I will not eat your meat. I do not understand your food," said Rattlesnake.

" What food do you eat? "

" I eat the yellow flowers of the corn."

Coyote at once began to search for the yellow corn flowers. When he found some, Rattlesnake said,

" Put some on top of my head so that I may eat it."

Coyote stood as far off as he could and placed the pollen on the snake's head.

The snake said, "Come nearer and put enough on my head so that I may find it."

Coyote was very much afraid, but after a while he came nearer and did as he was told.

Then the snake went away, saying,

"Companion, to-morrow you come to my house."

"All right," said Coyote. "To-morrow I will come."

Coyote sat down and thought about the morrow. He thought a good deal about what the snake might do. So he made a small rattle by placing tiny pebbles in a gourd and fastened it to the end of his tail. He shook it a while and was much pleased with it.

The next morning he started for the snake's house. He shook the rattle on the end of his tail and smiled, and said to himself,

"This is good. When I go into Rattlesnake's house, he will be very much afraid of me."

Coyote did not walk into Snake's house, but moved like a snake. But Coyote could not shake his rattle as the snake shook his. He had to hold it in his hand. But when he shook his rattle, the snake seemed much afraid, and said,

"Companion, I am afraid of you."

Now Rattlesnake had a stew of rats on the fire, and he placed some before Coyote. But Coyote said,

"I do not understand your food. I cannot eat it because I do not understand it."

Rattlesnake insisted upon his eating, but Coyote refused. He said,

"If you put some of the flower of the corn on my head, I will eat. I understand that food."

The snake took some corn pollen, but he pretended to be afraid of Coyote and stood off some distance. Coyote said,

"Come nearer and place it on top my head."

Snake replied, "I am afraid of you."

Coyote said, "Come nearer. I am not bad."

Then the snake came closer and put the pollen on top of Coyote's head.

But Coyote did not have the long tongue of the snake and he could not get the pollen off the top of his head. He put out his tongue first on one side of his nose and then on the other, but he could only reach to the side of his nose. His efforts made the snake laugh, but the snake put his hand over his mouth so Coyote should not see him laugh. Really, the snake hid his head in his body.

At last Coyote went home. As he left the snake's house, he held his tail in his hand and shook the rattle.

Snake cried, "Oh, companion! I am so afraid of you!" but really the snake shook with laughter.

When Coyote reached his home he said to himself, " I was such a fool. Rattlesnake had much food to eat and I would not take it. Now I am very hungry."

Then he went out in search of food.

ORIGIN OF THE SAGUARO AND PALO VERDE CACTI

Pima (*Arizona*)

ONCE upon a time an old Indian woman had two grandchildren. Every day she ground wheat and corn between the grinding stones to make porridge for them. One day as she put the water-olla on the fire outside the house to heat the water, she told the children not to quarrel because they might upset the olla. But the children began to quarrel. They upset the olla and spilled the water and their grandmother spanked them.

Then the children were angry and ran away. They ran far away over the mountains. The grandmother heard them whistling and she ran after them and followed them from place to place. but she could not catch up with them.

At last the older boy said, "I will turn into a saguaro, so that I shall live forever and bear fruit every summer."

The younger said, "Then I will turn into a palo verde and stand there forever. These mountains are

Department of Botanical Research of the Carnegie Institution of Washington

PALO VERDE CACTI

Pima Irrigation Dam

so bare and have nothing on them but rocks, I will make them green."

The old woman heard the cactus whistling and recognized the voice of her grandson. So she went up to it and tried to take the prickly thing into her arms, but the thorns killed her.

That is how the saguaro and the palo verde came to be on the mountains and the desert.

THE THIRSTY QUAILS

Pima (Arizona)

A QUAIL once had more than twenty children, and with them she wandered over the whole country in search of water and could not find it. It was very hot and they were all crying, "Where can we get some water? Where can we get some water?" but for a long time they could find none.

At last, way in the north, under a mesquite tree, the mother quail saw a pond of water, but it was very muddy and not fit to drink. But the little quails had been wandering so many days and were so tired they stopped under the shade of the mesquite tree, and by and by, one by one, they went down to the water and drank it. But the water was so bad they all died.

THE BOY AND THE BEAST

Pima (Arizona)

ONCE an old woman lived with her daughter and son-in-law and their little boy. They were following the trail of the Apache Indians. Now whenever a Pima Indian sees the trail of an Apache he draws a ring around it; then he can catch him sooner. And these Pimas drew circles around the trail of the Apaches they were following, but one night when they were asleep, the Apaches came down upon them. They took the man and younger woman by the hair and shook them out of their skins, just as one would shake corn out of a sack. So the boy and the old woman were left alone.

Now these two had to live on berries and anything they could find, and they wandered from place to place. In one place a strange beast, big enough to swallow people, camped in the bushes near them. The grandmother told the boy not to go near these bushes. But the boy took some sharp stones in his hands, and went toward them. As he came near, the great monster began to breathe. He began to suck in his breath and he sucked the boy right into his stomach. But with his sharp stones the boy began to cut the beast, so that he died. Then the boy made a hole large enough to climb out of.

When his grandmother came to look for him, the boy met her and said, "I have killed that monster."

The grandmother said, "Oh, no. Such a little boy as you are to kill such a great monster!"

The boy said, "But I was inside of him. Just look at the stones I cut him with."

Then the grandmother went softly up to the bushes, and looked at the monster. It was full of holes, just as the little boy had said.

Then they moved down among the berry bushes and had all they wanted to eat.

Putnam & Valentine

IN THE PETRIFIED FOREST OF ARIZONA

". . . threw all the Apaches over the mountains"

(Apache Basket-maker)

WHY THE APACHES ARE FIERCE

Pima (Arizona)

ELDER BROTHER, Coyote, and Earth Doctor, after the flood vanished, began to create people and animals. Coyote made all the animals, Elder Brother made the people, and Earth Doctor made queer creatures which had only one leg, or immense ears, or many fingers, and some having flames of fire in their knees.

Elder Brother divided his figures of people into four groups. One of the Apaches came to life first. He shivered and said, "Oh, it 's very cold," and began to sway back and forth. Then Elder Brother said, "I did n't think you would be the first to awake," and he took all the Apaches up in his hand and threw them over the mountains. That made them angry, and that is why they have always been so fierce.

SPEECH ON THE WARPATH

Pima (Arizona)

WE have come thus far, my brothers. In the east there is White Gopher, who gnaws with his strong teeth. He was friendly and came to me. On his way he came to the surface from the underground four times. Looking in all four directions, he saw a magic whitish trail. Slowly following this, he neared the enemy, coming to the surface from the underground four times during the journey. Their power stood in their land like a mountain, but he bit it off short, and he sank their springs by biting them. He saw that the wind of the enemy was strong and he cut it up with his teeth. He gnawed in short pieces their clouds. They had good dreams and bright false-seeing, good bow strings and straight-flying reeds, but these he grasped and bit off short. The different belongings lying about he took with him, turning around homeward. On his way homeward over the whitish trail, he came to the surface four times, and magic fire appeared around the edges. Then he came to his bed. He felt that the land roared rejoicingly with him.

In the south was Blue Coyote and there I sent my cry. He was friendly and came to me from his blue darkness, circling around and shouting, four times, on his journey, making magic fire everywhere. When he arrived, he looked in four directions, then understood. A whitish magic trail lay before him. He cast his blue darkness upon the enemy and slowly approached them, circling around and shouting four times on the way. Like a mountain was their power in the land, and he sucked it in. The springs of water under the trees he sucked in. The wind that was blowing he inhaled. He sucked in the clouds. The people dreamed of a white thing, and their dreams he sucked in, with their best bow strings and the straight-flying reeds. All the different belongings which lay around he gathered and slowly turned back. Hidden in the blue darkness, he came to me, circling around, shouting, four times on his journey. Then he homeward took his way, circling, howling, four times, and shouting reached his bed. With pleasure he felt all directions *thud.* The east echoed.

In the sunset direction was Black Kangaroo Mouse, an expert robber. To him I sent my cry. He was friendly to me and came hidden in black darkness, sitting down four times upon his way. Magic fire covered the edges of his trail. When he reached me, he looked in all directions. The magic trail brightly lay before him. He threw black darkness around him and slowly reached the enemy, sitting down four times upon the trail. He found a bag of the enemy, with much prized possessions. It was tied one knot on top of another, but he bit them off. He took from it the blue necklaces, blue earrings, and the different belongings lying around gathered up with him. Then he slowly took his way back on the magic trail, with magic fire everywhere. Hidden in his yellow darkness, he returned to me. He left the others at the council and in darkness took his homeward way, resting four times. He sat on his bed and felt all directions of the earth rustling in the darkness. Darkness lay all around.

I called on Owl, the white blood-sucker. To him I sent my cry. He was friendly and came down to me with four thin flys (sailing) on the way. He looked in all directions. The magic trail brightly before him lay. He flew, with four thin flys, toward the enemy. The mountain of their power which stood in the land he bit off short. The springs he bit off, and their very good dreams. The best bow strings and the straight-flying reeds he grasped and cut very short. He bit off their flesh and made holes in their bones. From the things gathered, he made a belt from a bowstring. Then he returned. He came through the whitish mist of dawn in four flights. The people held a council. Leaving them there, he after four thin flys reached his bed in the gray dawn mist. Then in all directions he heard the darkness rattling, as he lay there.

THE SPIRIT LAND

Gallinomero (Russian River, Cal.)

WHEN the flames burn low on the funeral pyres of the Gallinomero, Indian mourners gather up handfuls of ashes and scatter them high in air. Thus the good mount up into the air, or go to the Happy Western Land beyond the Big Water.

But the bad Indians go to an island in the Bitter Waters, an island naked and barren and desolate, covered only with brine-spattered stone, swept with cold winds and the biting sea-spray. Here they live always, breaking stone upon one another, with no food but the broken stones and no drink but the salt sea water.

Putnam & Valentine

"Bad Indians go to an island in the Bitter Waters"

Courtesy of F. Ellerman, Mount Wilson Solar Observatory

"The giant Sierras, fringed at the base with dark pines"

SONG OF THE GHOST DANCE

Pai Ute (Kern River, Cal.)

The snow lies there — *ro-rani!*
The snow lies there — *ro-rani!*
The snow lies there — *ro-rani!*
The snow lies there — *ro-rani!*
The Milky Way lies there.
The Milky Way lies there.

"This is one of the favorite songs of the Paiute Ghost dance. . . . It must be remembered that the dance is held in the open air at night, with the stars shining down on the wide-extending plain walled in by the giant Sierras, fringed at the base with dark pines, and with their peaks white with eternal snows. Under such circumstances this song of the snow lying white upon the mountains, and the Milky Way stretching across the clear sky, brings up to the Paiute the same patriotic home love that comes from lyrics of singing birds and leafy trees and still waters to the people of more favored regions. . . . The Milky Way is the road of the dead to the spirit world."

THE END